The development of modern Turkey as measured by its press

Ahmet Emin Yalman

1

THE DEVELOPMENT OF MODERN TURKEY
AS MEASURED BY ITS PRESS

STUDIES IN HISTORY, ECONOMICS AND PUBLIC LAW

EDITED BY THE FACULTY OF POLITICAL SCIENCE
OF COLUMBIA UNIVERSITY

Volume LIX]   [Number 1

Whole Number 142

THE DEVELOPMENT OF MODERN TURKEY AS MEASURED BY ITS PRESS

BY

AHMED EMIN, Ph.D.,

New York
COLUMBIA UNIVERSITY
LONGMANS, GREEN & CO., AGENTS
LONDON: P. S. KING & SON

1914

PREFACE

MUCH has been written in western languages on decaying Turkey, on Turkey as a spoil to be divided among foreign powers, but very little on Turkey developing and striving to develop.

An attempt only is made in the following pages to give a view of Turkey in her struggle for survival and for betterment. The press has been selected as an index and measure, because it has always been the leading factor in the Modern Turkish movement, because also the writer is personally acquainted with that field.

AHMED EMIN.

NEW YORK, FEBRUARY, 1914.

CONTENTS

CHAPTER IV

THE HAMIDIAN PERIOD

CHAPTER V

THE PRESENT ERA

Part I Developments since 1908 and their interpretation

CHAPTER I

INTRODUCTION

FEW countries can compete in the making of history with the wide territories, now under the rule of the government of Constantinople. Owing to their extended coast line, their central position and their resources, they always were an active field for the movements of populations, for the conflicts of races and cultures, for the accumulation and combination of ideas. The products of this perpetual historical process could not be subjected to a general amalgamation. Under the protection of different environmental influences in the various parts of these territories different physical types, different kinds and epochs of culture, different languages could survive side by side.

On these, the Turks had a foundation of doubtful sociological value on which to build up an empire. Indeed, when one closely realizes the heterogeneity of the conditions they found in Asia Minor and Southeastern Europe, one cannot help asking: How was the whole thing possible? How could a great empire be built up on such a basis and maintained for more than six centuries? One becomes more and more puzzled by remembering that the founders of the Ottoman Empire were but a fraction of a single wandering Turkish tribe, and had to face, for many generations, a keen antagonism from all stocks kindred to them, religiously or racially, instead of support and help.

A task of such tremendous delicacy could not be solved by sword merely. A very efficient organization was necessary This the founders of the empire succeeded in creating. The iron sense of discipline they brought from Central Asia was a good equipment for their work. They further found in Mohammedanism a machine for assimilation and a source of solidarity. A third favorable factor was the vast opportunity for the selection of ideas and people. The air of the frontier region, where the foundation of the new empire was laid, was filled with tried ideas of government handed down for centuries, from people to people, from generation to generation. Not only was a successful selection made from this large store of ideas, but also the best people from the neighboring or subjected stocks were selected and trained through ingenious methods, to carry them out.[1]

The system based upon these foundations enabled the early Turks to form a new and compact nation out of heterogeneous elements within a few generations and to extend their frontiers with extraordinary rapidity. They laid such a strong foundation for the structure that it could withstand the greatest shocks and crises for centuries, and disprove over and over again the prophecies as to its undelayable end.

The system itself was too artificial to maintain its efficiency forever. Rapid growth, easy success, accumulation of wealth by conquest with corresponding love of luxury had in themselves elements of degeneracy. Besides, the best point in the system contained a germ of destruction. In order to prevent the conquering race from living as parasites on the state body, and from forming a privileged hereditary class, at the expense of the power of the Crown, the offices in the army and the executive were regularly filled with specially trained Christian converts. The children of these converts were considered members of the rul-

[1] A clear description of the system may be found in Professor L. H. Lybyer's *The Government of the Ottoman Empire in the Time of Suleiman the Magnificent,* Harvard University Press, 1913.

ing Turkish race and could not hold office. The Turks, *i. e.* Turkish-speaking Mohammedans, were thus forced to devote their attention to agriculture, industry, commerce, or to careers of learning. All this was admirably planned, but it produced a large debarred and discontented class, ready to do away, at the first opportunity, with the barriers to their advancement

And so it happened. Selim II and Mourad III who succeeded Suleiman the Magnificent (1520-1566), the great conquering and organizing Sultan, on the Ottoman throne, were men of weak disposition. They lacked the qualities of leadership necessary to run the complex governmental machinery. The joints began to be loosened. The members of the conquering race gradually invaded the government offices and the army, without going through the severe special training. Evils like favoritism, palace intrigues, weakening of the central authority, artificially kept away until then, made their appearance. The skillful scheme of selection which meant for the ruling race an addition of good blood at the expense of subjected races ceased and the Mohammendan, and especially the Turkish part of the population had alone to bear the cost in life of the almost constant wars.

Among other beneficial features of the old system, the machinery for change and readjustment was also destroyed. In the face of external dangers which put an end to aggressive action and invasion, and made the country assume a defensive position, the religious class acquired more and more prestige, with the result that change and betterment came into disrepute, and everything became crystallized and stationary.

The shifting of the world's trade and communication from the Mediteranean to Western Europe through Da Gama's voyage around the Cape of Good Hope gave an additional blow to the Ottoman Empire.

Still, there were attempts made for betterment, as often as matters became too critical. The foundation originally laid was so solid that a strong man was always able to put the machinery in order and run it smoothly for a while. As there were no hereditary rights, and as even in the times of greatest degeneracy and decay, a man of humble origin but strong will, could work his way up to the top, a relatively great productivity in strong leaders was noticeable in all periods of urgent need. With them the empire rose and fell. In view of the internal situation and of constant external dangers, however, their efforts could not exceed the limits of a struggle for mere survival.

It can hardly be surmised what course Ottoman history would have taken amidst these ups and downs, had the Western world not ushered in an era entirely new in human evolution.

The changes in the West, combined with repeated misfortune in war began to stimulate in Turkey, conscious efforts to save the country from decay by adopting some of the Western ways. The first great success along this line was achieved, when, with government help, a printing press was established in Constantinople in 1140 A. H. (1728).

The conflict between the old and the new has continued ever since. In the latter half of the eighteenth and the first half of the nineteenth centuries the reform movement was carried out by enlightened Sultans, in particular Mahmoud II, and their ministers. After the annihilation in 1825 of the *janissaries*, a military corps which had effectually opposed any kind of change and any betterment for generations, the course of progress became more and more rapid. The face of Turkey changed so radically that Lord Palmerston could say in 1856: " In the last thirty years Turkey has made greater progress than any nation of Europe ".

The reforms however, hardly constituted a real adjustment to new conditions. They were mostly dictated by the pressure of the moment and by the instinct of self-preservation. The state of affairs was far from pleasing to the new generation of idealists and patriots. They saw in democracy, a panacea for regenerating the country, and engaged in a vigorous struggle for obtaining a constitution.

In 1876, when the reformers seemed to have finally reached their goal, Sultan Abdul Hamid appeared on the scene. His well organized autocratic system did away with many possibilities of development and improvement, but created, in ways of opposition, new nationalistic tendencies and collective efforts for self-realization. In spite of the large number of martyrs, the revolutionary movement was kept alive in foreign countries and triumphed in 1908.

When the veil, imposed by a despotic government was removed, a sad picture revealed itself. It was a picture of chaos, of degeneracy, of disintegration. With a part of the population directly hostile to the very existence of the empire, another large part indifferent, and those interested in the destinies of the country lacking in deliberative like-mindedness and solidarity, a liberal constitution could hardly play the part of a panacea and transform this picture immediately into one of harmony and progress, as the Turkish idealist hoped. An era of dangerous experimenting, but of brave desire for improvement, began, interrupted by the array of external difficulties expressly created by Russia and some other powers, wishing for their own interests only a weak and decaying Turkey.

As long as the external dangers kept the general attention and the largest part of the empire's energy had to be devoted to the maintenance of order in and the defense of European Turkey, the rapid changes taking place in every branch of Turkish life could not go beneath the form and surface, and meant in the long run mere destruction and annihilation instead of improvement.

The recent misfortune in the Balkan War and the accompanying amputation of the sick and energy-absorbing parts of territory have changed the whole outlook. Freed from the most dangerous part of her imperial burden, Turkey may now freely look forward to an era of democratic development.

The Turkish press which will be studied in the following pages is the factor which, in the last instance, did most to prepare the ground for the present situation in Turkey.

The press began, as has everything modern in Turkey, as a government institution, and maintained this character until 1860. When an independent class of reformers and innovators arose, it passed under their control and had its golden period at their hands, between 1860 and 1876. After his accession to the throne, Sultan Abdul Hamid (1876) did everything to reduce it to a mere tool of his will and to a prop of his system. As a result, the real press activity and free intellectual life of Turkey transferred itself to France, Egypt, and other places, and from there, furnished the country, artificially isolated, with an underground life-stream. Since the proclamation of the constitution, the press has enjoyed a status, incomparably better than the previous state of affairs. It has at least been able to play, on the general social field, a free part in leadership, and to act as an unrestricted intermediary of ideas between Turkey and the Western World. There has been a tendency, however, altering in degree with the constant political changes, towards repressing adverse political criticism. The last phase of development, as indicated by the creation of eleven weeklies for schools and children and five weeklies on farming, is a sound specialization in periodicals. The dailies which are decreasing in number, but increasing in circulation, have also ceased to be elements of contest and agitation, standing and working for stability.

CHAPTER II

THE PRE-JOURNALISTIC PERIOD

THE dawn of the newspaper era in Turkey is a comparatively recent event. It dates back only to the second quarter of the nineteenth century. Previous to that time, there were ways and means to discharge some of the functions of the press, which originated mainly in certain peculiarities of Turkish social life

The social life of Turkey provided for an abundant amount of intercourse: the mosque, with its five daily and extra-Friday meetings, the convent of the *dervishes*, the coffee-house, the market-place, the *caravanseray*, all served to bring and to keep people constantly in communication. In addition, the Turkish traditions of limitless hospitality afforded opportunity to every class of people to intermingle and associate with each other very closely and intimately. As an outcome, what one knew or thought could easily become common knowledge. This freedom of intercourse and communication may explain in a measure, why so many fierce mob outbreaks played so large a part in Turkish history, although the individuals themselves were of a rather peaceful and quiet disposition.

On occasions, when some party deliberately desired to diffuse certain news, or the government wanted to make certain announcements, the usual medium was the public crier. In the interior of Asia Minor and even in some of the larger coast towns, this custom still survives, although now, every province has its official weekly, and many of the provinces have non-official weeklies and dailies. Formerly, imperial and local laws and regulations were announced through public criers on the market place and in the adjoining streets. The same medium was used to publish great military news, or the appointment and date of arrival of a new provincial governor, or the fixed date of religious festivals, as well as the announcement of the death of a prominent man, and the arrival or departure of caravans or ships

The public crier was especially important as an advertising agency. He had to make announcements regarding the farming of government revenues, lost articles, missing persons, escaped convicts, articles to be sold and meetings to be held. In Constantinople, the only surviving trace of this system at the present time, is the announcement on the streets of the breaking out of a fire.

In matters which were to be announced by the authorities to the non-Mohammedan parts of the population alone, there was no need for the public crier. In the case of these, the government maintained the principle of a collective community responsibility, and restricted itself to making announcements to the heads of the respective communities. The official historiographer Wassif, who had to deal with the period between 1753 and 1774, gives the following example of this: [1]

As the Greek, Armenian and Jewish people living in Constantinople had gone beyond the lawful limits in their dressing the Greek and Armenian patriarchs and the community-head of the Jewish people were summoned to the seat of the *tchavoush-bashi agha* (the chief of police). The sublime order, issued to the effect that they should arrange their dress according to the old style, was communicated to all of them. They were threatened and warned, one by one, through the state-

---

[1] *Tarikhi-Vassif* (Boulak Edition, Cairo, 1830), vol. i, p. 67.

ment that going beyond the limits would result in most vigorous punishment.

The spreading of opinions and the moulding of news
were principally the business of religious preachers.   Especially in the fasting month of *Ramazan* and the two
months preceding, it was customary for theological students and many other members of the religious profession
to wander from place to place preaching on current topics.
They did not, however, constitute a well trained and well
organized force, which might be purposefully managed and
directed.   It is interesting to note here that the official
historiographer Na'ima, who had to deal with the period
between 1592 and 1659, advocates, among other measures
which he suggests for a general improvement of the conditions of the empire, making good use of the preachers.
He says: [1]

. . . Even the most majestic buildings are bound to decay.
Therefore, attention must be given to raise men before all.
People of initiative and activity must be encouraged.   The
hearth of public spirit of the people must be kept afire.   It is
necessary for this purpose to send able preachers among the
people.   They ought to urge them in times of peace, to work
and to be tranquil and orderly.   In times of war, they ought
to call meetings and incite the people by relating in a forceful
speech the deeds of their forefathers and other appropriate
stories. . . .

Na'ima does not forget the importance of the written
word.   He urges the wise and learned to write pamphlets
with a view to enlightening the people, and then he advises
the government never to overlook an effort of this sort but
to reward it as highly as it deserves.

[1] *Tarikhi-Na'ima* (Constantinople, 1734), vol. i, p. 31.

It is not easy to test the degree of influence of the spoken word in the pre-journalistic era   There can be no doubt, however, regarding the importance of the written word. Everything written was considered wellnigh sacred, and writers of every class were highly respected.   The Hollander Anger Busbeck, (1522-92) who visited Constantinople in 1555, as the envoy of King Ferdinand of Hungary, remarked that everyone took great care in picking up any pieces of paper from the floor, lest somebody step on them. It was a pious deed for a wealthy man to establish a public library.   *Centralblatt für Bibliothekwesen,* no. 6, 1907,[1] speaks of ninety thousand men who made a living by copying books, before the printing press was instituted.

It is noteworthy that, in spite of the general love for books and in spite of the fact that copied books were so expensive, the printing press was introduced as late as 1728. There was, however, a Jewish printing office in Constantinople at the end of the fifteenth century, and several Greek and Armenian offices in 1628.[2]   The fact that the Turks did not seem to be aware of them, illustrates plainly how independently from each other the different elements of population in Turkey lived.

Moreover, a trustworthy historian like Moustafa Pasha relates [3] that during the reign of Murad III (1574-1595) permission was given to a foreigner to import a press to Turkey and to print Turkish books.   This press was even exempted from import duty.   Moustafa Pasha pretends to have seen in the library of the *Sheikh-ul-Islam* Hassam

---

[1] This statement is based upon the observations of Marsigli, *Stato militare dell'Imperio Ottomano,* Bibliothèque française, xvii, 1732, pp 313, 314

[2] Ubicini, *Letters on Turkey* (London, 1826), vol. i, p. 235.

[3] *Netaij-ul-vukuhat.* (Results of Events), second edition (Constantinople, 1911), vol iii, p. 110.

Effendi, a Turkish book printed in 996 A. H. (1588). If true, this report illustrates the attitude maintained towards change both in the rise and decay periods of Turkish history. It seems that in the period of rise and growth, when the military class had the lead, an innovation of such magnitude could be introduced on mere secular authority, without obtaining the sanction of the high juris-consult in canon law. In the period of decay, on the other hand, when supremacy had passed over to the religious class, great opposition was made against the introduction of any such European invention. It was only through the threats of the enlightened Grand Vezir Ibrahim Pasha that the religious authorities could be induced to give their consent to the establishment of a Turkish printing press.

Ibrahim Pasha's time was one of quiet and peace. He purposefully avoided wars in spite of the provocation offered by the European situation, and devoted his attention to matters of learning and art. Among other improvements, he established a public library in 1719.

In the same year, he instructed Tchelebi Mehmed Effendi [1] who was going to Paris as a special envoy " to become acquainted with the conditions of progress and learning in France and to report on those phases of them which were applicable in Turkey."

Mehmed Effendi was accompanied on his trip by his son Saïd Effendi. The young man was above all impressed by the advantages of printing and ascribed to them the rapid progress made in Europe. He decided at once to introduce it in Turkey. The official historiographer of the period, Assimme Effendi, gives this account of the matter: [2]

---

[1] *Mehmed Effendi's account of his trip,* Ebouz-Zia Edition (Constantinople, 1306 [1890]), p. 4.

[2] Abdurahman Sheref, *Tarikhi-Devleti-Osmania* (Constantinople, second edition, 1900), vol. ii, p. 153.

... It became clear in the penetrating eyes of Saïd Effendi that the Frank people who are the devils of the human species were making easy the achievement of many a difficult matter by using the tools of thought and imagination   It remained specially fixed on the pages of his mind that they could produce several hundreds of illustrious books in a short time through the art of printing and multiplying.   That created in him the wish of spreading this desirable art in the paradise-like Turkish territories and to increase the number of rare and expensive books which constitute the instruments of higher learning.

Saïd Effendi found a capable co-worker in the person of a Hungarian renegade named Ibrahim Effendi.[1]   Together they drew up an elaborate memoir detailing the benefits of printing   This memoir was presented to the Sultan through the Grand Vezir Ibrahim Pasha.

At the first rumor of the proposed innovation alarm spread throughout Constantinople.   The many thousands of scribes, living by copying books saw their profession in peril   The theologians found the new project profane; the emanations of human intelligence, they alleged, having always been handed down to posterity by writing, ought not to be subjected to any less carefully made transmission.   A third party, the scholars and those who cherished literature for its own sake, were disturbed by fears lest the precious art of caligraphy, which shed glory even on the noblest thoughts, by the beauteous lines and marvelous symbolical interlacings of the letters and ciphers it employed in expressing them, should be lost to mankind

" Notwithstanding all opposition, however, the result took place which will invariably occur in Turkey, whenever an energetic and enlightened sovereign is supported by a Grand Vezir and a Sheikh-ul-Islam capable of compre-

[1] There is now a movement set afoot in Turkey by *the friends of the City of Constantinople* to erect a mausoleum for Ibrahim Effendi.

hending and assisting his views." [1]   The copyists were silenced by the promise that the government would not allow the printing of religious books, and that it would support them in need.   The means resorted to for checking the fanatical opposition was to obtain a *fatva* from *Sheikh-ul-Islam* Abdullah Effendi to the effect that the innovation was in accordance with the canon law and religious principles.

A *fatva* is an opinion or decision as to requirements of the canon law, formally given on an abstruse case of law by an officer duly appointed for the purpose.   A *fatva* specially issued by the *Sheikh-ul-Islam* is of aboslute effect, and means, both in a legal and religious way, immediate social sanction.   It must be remembered that the three last Sultans of Turkey lost their throne as a result of a *fatva*.   A *fatva* gave Sultan Mahmoud II the power to dissolve the whole military corps of *janissaries*.

The *fatva* in the case of the printing press,[2] was this:

Question — If Zaid,[3] who pretends to have ability in the art of printing says that he can engrave on molds the figures of letters and words of books edited on language, logic, philosophy, astronomy and similar secular subjects, and produce copies of such books by pressing the paper on the molds, is the practice of such a process of printing permissible to Zaid by canon law.   An opinion is asked on this matter.

Answer—God knows it best.   If a person who has ability in the art of printing engraves the letters and words of a corrected book correctly on a mold and produces many copies without difficulty in a short time by pressing the paper on that mold, the abundance of books might cheapen the price and result in their increased purchase.   This being a tremendous

---

[1] Ubicini, *op. cit.*, p. 237.

[2] Abdurahman Sheref, *op. cit.*, vol. ii, pp. 153, 154.

[3] *Zaid* and *Amr* are the *Caius* and *Sempronius* of Mohammedan law

benefit, the matter is a highly laudable one. Permission should be granted to that person, but some learned persons should be appointed to correct the book the figures of which are to be engraved.

Upon this, the imperial mandate of July 5, 1727, was issued sanctioning the printing of books and appointing four censors to supervise the working of the printing office.

The first book printed was an Arabic-Turkish Dictionary. It contained the text of the *fatva,* and articles written by several persons of learning, high in the religious hierarchy, on the benefits of printing [1]

The books printed within the first three decades were not large in number. In 1756, twenty-nine years after the foundation of the establishment, only eighteen works, forming twenty-five volumes had been printed. Of these, sixteen thousand five hundred copies in all were issued, the prices of which, fixed by the government, varied from $8 to $17 each, American money.

According to Ubicini,[2] the price of an ordinary folio manuscript at the time, without ornament or illuminations varied from thirty to thirty-six pounds sterling. Copies of the Koran from the pen of Hafiz Osman or any equally celebrated transcriber in Nessik caligraphy, were two hundred to two hundred-fifty pounds.

Owing to the deaths of the initiators and their pupils, and to the continuous and disastrous wars, the printing press was neglected from 1756 to 1783 In 1784, it was re-established as the result of an imperial order.

Hammer and Bianchi [3] give a catalogue of all the works

---

[1] *Tarikhi-Djevdet* (Constantinople, 1855-84), vol. i, special chapter on printing.

[2] Ubicini, *op. cit*, vol. i, p. 238.

[3] Hammer, *History of the Ottoman Empire* (French Edition), vol. xiv. Bianchi, appendix to his *Notice of a Treatise on Anatomy, by Chain Zadeh*

published up to the year 1828. They consisted of eighty works, forming ninety-one volumes. Among them in numbers, history and geography came first with eighteen volumes. Sixteen volumes were devoted to language, fourteen to religion, thirteen to mathematics, astronomy and medicine, eleven to jurisprudence, four to rhetoric, three to military scubjects, and two to metaphysics. The rest were publications connected with the administration of government. After the reform of Mahmoud II, the number of publications suddenly increased, amounting to one hundred and eight works between 1830 and 1842. On the other hand, the printing establishment of Boulak, founded in Egypt in 1821, by Mehmed Ali Pasha, had published in the first twenty years of its existence two hundred and forty-three works in Turkish, Arabic and Persian.[1]

There was also a separate establishment at Constantinople for the translation and publication of all works relating to the theory and practice of the art of war.

It is striking that no books of imaginative and purely literary character were published for more than a century after the institution of printing, although collections of poetry used to form a prominent feature on Turkish book shelves. This may be explained by the fact that the printing press was at first a purely governmental institution and had to be used systematically as an agent of enlightenment and progress The pressing character of the time did not allow the reformers to go beyond practical considerations or to give attention to aesthetic pleasure and literary amusement.

According to the Turkish Historian, Abdurahman Sheref,[2] the effect of the distribution of books by means

---

[1] A complete catalogue by Bianchi, Paris, 1843.

[2] *Op. cit.*, vol. ii, p. 57.

of printing was great and immediate. " The books first printed were mostly on history and geography They gave serenity to the mind and enabled people to interpret the present through the events of the past, and to foresee the future This and the intercourse with European envoys and ministers brought about at least among the people of distinction, an appreciation for new inventions and esteem and sympathy for the European civilization "

One of the results of this change of attitude was the establishment of a press bureau, where the most important European papers were read and the parts of interest translated The translations were often carefully conserved in the archives as historical documents. The historian Jevdet Pasha in his books repeatedly makes use of such documents. For the purpose of this bureau, Frederick the Great of Prussia was asked to give the names of two papers which might keep Turkey in touch with the real state of affairs in Europe. Frederick promptly recommended *La Gazette de Clèves* and *Le Courrier du Bas-Rhin*, which not only were inspired by him constantly, but were furnished with articles written by himself, as well, on international politics [1]

In spite of the appreciation of the power of the press, manifested in the establishment of a press bureau, no attempt was made until 1831 to publish a Turkish paper. In the old order of things there was simply no need and no place for a paper. It came after Mahmoud II had established, at least in form, a new order of things, and after new ideas of government were embodied in Turkish life as a consequence of Western influences.

---

[1] Zinkeisen, *Geschichte des osmanischen Reiches in Europe*, vol. vi, pp. 290-291. Hamburg, 1840-63.

CHAPTER III

The Era of Genesis

SULTAN MAHMOUD II, (1808-1839) is a very interesting figure in Turkish history. He came to the throne of Turkey in a most critical time. The empire was in rapid process of dissolution. The attempts of Selim III at reform had ended in his being murdered. The capital was dominated by a reactionary mob of *janissaries*. The provinces had become semi-independent.

The young Sultan bravely took up a single-handed struggle against the existing abuses and prejudices. He cleared the way for reforms by destroying the *janissaries* and the semi-feudal system in the provinces. He succeeded in building a modern structure on the old ground. It is true that this was only a superficial imitation of the Western systems, and that it remained to a great extent only on paper or in name and form. But still, considered in the light of the previous conditions, Mahmoud's work was really amazing.

In his efforts to modernize Turkey, he saw the necessity of securing the support and co-operation of his people. One of the most important steps he took in this direction was the founding of a newspaper.

Sultan Mahmoud's paper was, however, neither the first paper published in Turkey, nor the first periodical publication in the Turkish language. The first Turkish periodical was the Turkish-Arabic semi-weekly, established on November 20, 1828, in Egypt, by Mehmed Ali Pasha.[1]

[1] *Journal Asiatique*, 1831, vol. xix, p. 231.

27]

27

Verminhac, French minister to Constantinople, had published in 1795, a French *Gazette* for some time   In 1811, the French legation issued bulletins on the movements of Napoleon.[1]

The first real newspaper was the *Spectateur de l'Orient,* established in 1825 at Smyrna, by a Frenchman named Alexandre Blacque. This paper, the name of which was later changed to the *Courrier de Smyrne,* proved itself of great service to Turkey by defending her interests during the international complications of the time, especially during the Greek revolt. In this connection it often took occasion to attack vigorously the policy of Russia. The Russian ambassador, becoming extremely alarmed, made remonstrances to theSublime Porte on the subject.[2]

The Porte however, took an evasive attitude, promising much and doing little. Repeated discussions took place in this regard between the ambassador and Akif Pasha, the Minister for Foreign Affairs. In one of them, the envoy of Russia used the following argument.

It is true that in France and England journalists are free to write anything, even against their kings. But it is also true that in former times, several wars were caused between England and France by the newspapers. Praise be to God, the Ottoman Empire was saved from this evil, until that man appeared in Smyrna, and began to publish his paper. It would be very wise to stop him. I am free to go about naked in my house, but if I go to the street in that way, I am immediately arrested as a lunatic. Similarly, that French journalist may express himself freely in his own country, but must be pre-

[1] Ubicini and Courteille, *Etat présent de l'Empire Ottomane* (Paris, 1876), pp. 167 ff.

[2] The whole incident is related in A. Lutfi's annals, vol. iii, p. 98, Constantinople, 1874-86.

vented from doing so, and from attacking friendly powers when he is in Turkey.

Instead of satisfying Russia, the Turkish government during the very year of this diplomatic incident, invited Mr. Blacque to publish in Constantinople, and in the French language, an official paper, with a view of defending the interests of the Empire. The paper was called *Moniteur Ottoman*, and was followed the next year by the *Takvimi-Vekayih*, the first Turkish paper in Turkey.

Sultan Mahmoud's order of 1247 (1832) regarding the establishment of a newspaper was in the following terms:

> . . . The publication of a newspaper was for me an ideal for a very long time. But as the time was not yet ripe, I preferred to wait for the proper moment. As the time is now ripe, and as the matter does not harm our laws and religion, and is willingly recommended by everybody to be highly beneficial, we desire to proceed to the establishment of a newspaper. . . .

A list of suggested names was presented to the Sultan all of which he passed over, but he devised himself the name of *Takvimi-Vekayih* (The Calendar of Events). It appeared under this name on May 14, 1832.

The first number contained a leading article which was written to justify for a newspaper the right of existence. It is striking that the article does not even allude to the progress of the press in Europe, and to the existence of the Turkish paper in Egypt, or to the French papers in Turkey. It simply represents the publication of a newspaper as the logical continuation of the old Turkish tradition of employing official historiographers to publish at regular intervals, historical annals

The article says in part:

To know the events of the past serves to keep up the laws and the character of the Empire and the solidarity of the nation. It is for this purpose that the government has always employed historiographers and published historical works.

However, if the daily events are not made public at the time of their occurrence, and their true nature is not disclosed, the people are apt to interpret governmental acts in ways which are not even dreamed of or imagined by the authors. Human nature is always inclined to attack and criticize everything, the character and truth of which it does not know In order to check the attacks and misunderstandings and to give people rest of mind, and satisfaction, it is necessary to make them acquainted with the real nature of events. It would also be a useful thing for the people and a beneficial act for the empire and nation to make public facts on sciences, fine arts and trade. It would be difficult to do this work of publication day by day by mere handwriting. The easy way would be to use a press, similar to the one already existing in the imperial capital.

As the kindness of His Majesty regarding all his subjects, and his good will to all friendly powers are evident, the utility of the work will be extended to them by making publications in languages other than Turkish. It has been decided to employ for this purpose a reliable foreign refugee.

The paper will comprise two parts. The first will contain official communications concerning internal affairs, and the second unofficial news, educational, scientific, industrial and commercial articles and a record of events, appearing in the " Mirror of the Universe" according to times and circumstances

The Sultan took great interest in the paper. He directed its policy and gave attention even to details in its style. On the occasion of his trip to Varna, the editor of the paper, had written a long note in the old official style. Upon this, the following imperial order was issued: [1]

---

[1] A Lutfi, *op. cit*, vol. iv, p. 90.

It cannot be denied that the note was well and masterfully written. Care must be taken, however, that matters of this kind addressed to the people at large should be edited in a popular style, and should contain only words and terms intelligible to everybody.

Then, the Sultan proceeded to enumerate the words in the note in question which a popular publication should not use. The Sultan himself used simple and paternal language in all his communications to the functionaries.

Sultan Mahmoud's newspaper began its business life in a very peculiar way. Instead of seeking subscribers, "a list was made of all state officials, people of learning, and notables, both in the capital and in the provinces, as well as of foreign ambassadors and ministers, and mostly all of the five thousand copies printed, were distributed according to that list "[1] As the post service was organized during the same year, it may fairly be assumed that this was stimulated by the necessity of sending off the thousands of newspaper copies every week.

The attitude taken by official Europe towards the importation of journalism in Turkey is illustrated by the following lines written in 1853:[2]

The beginnings of journalism in Turkey at first passed unregarded, or were considered as abortive efforts which would quickly expire of themselves, but when it was seen that they daily grew in strength and importance and were taking a firm root in the country, great uneasiness began to manifest itself amongst the European missions and embassies at Pera; partly from the dislike with which every tendency to Turkish reform and improvement was beheld by certain parties, partly from the jealousy which these missions always entertained of each

[1] A. Lutfi, *op. cit.*, vol. iii, p. 156.
[2] M A. Ubicini, *op. cit.*, p. 247.

other's influence, and which on the present occasion they united in entertaining towards that of France.

Secret intrigues and open opposition were employed to crush and annihilate the rising innovation. Some even affecting a display of alarm and uneasiness for the consequences to the Turkish government, addressed notes of warning and remonstrance to the Porte, but happily, in this instance, Sultan Mahmoud, relying on his own strength, turned a deaf ear to the representations of his European friends.

For some time, *Takvimi-vacayih* remained, with the exception of the almanac of the court astrologer, the only Turkish periodic publication. In 1843, an Englishman, Mr. N. Churchill by name, established the *Djeridei-Havadis* (Register of News) a Turkish weekly (later issued five times a week), which was devoted chiefly to foreign politics. According to Ubicini,[1] this paper, as well as several French papers, received an annual subvention of about fourteen hundred dollars.

In spite of the restriction involved in governmental support and the embarrassment caused by the interference of foreign embassies, the small number of papers had a revolutionizing effect. Ubicini, who wrote his book before the Crimean War, says:[2]

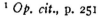

If we compare the state of things in Turkey thirty years ago with what it is at the present day, we shall be struck with the wonderful change, and this change, this progress, this recognition of many of the advantages which Western nations possess, giving rise as it naturally does, to a desire to acquire their languages, their arts and their science—all that heretofore was ignored and despised, now justly appreciated—has it not been brought about in a great measure by the influence of the press?

[1] *Op. cit.*, p. 251   [2] *Ibid.*, p. 252.

The Crimean War and the general eagerness to get war news gave a new turn to the position of the press, extending the circle of readers and making the ground ready for self-supporting and independent newspapers. Papers of this type were bound to come soon, because there was a new movement afoot, a spirit of dissent and revolt, which needed expression. Hitherto, most of the reforms in Turkey were made under the pressure of dangerous situations, and they formed a structure modern in form, but loose and without coördination. A by-product of the reform era was a new type of young men, who were sincere but over-zealous patriots, nationalists, instead of religious fanatics. They wanted to save Turkey from decay by awakening a new national consciousness and ending foreign interventions and intrigues. The method they devised for attaining this was simple: it was to adopt the most progressive system of government, and the most advanced European laws. This naïve radicalism which is common to all subsequent periods of Turkish history, as well as to the reformers of all backward countries, had a great advantage: it made the discontented and radical elements keep more or less united in the struggle towards a common goal —at least as long as they had something to oppose. As early as 1858, the young idealists organized a conspiracy under the direction of a general named Husni Pasha, to secure the proclamation of a parliamentary system of government.[1] Those who took part in it were so numerous that the plans could not be kept secret for any length of time and the attempt failed, but the spirit which had fostered it gained strength in spite of this failure. As a result of the close contact with Europeans during the Crimean War, everybody, even every class of religious dignitaries, hitherto opposed

[1] Ed. Englehardt, *La Turque et le Tanzimat,* vol. i, p. 158, Paris, 1882.

to change, had the feeling that something big and great
had to be done for the future of the country.   Pamphlets
advocating reforms and using the progress of Europe as an
argument found wide circulation.   Societies of different
kinds were formed, and the coffee house, that important
Turkish institution, gained more and more the character
of a literary and political club

It was in this time of animation and militancy that the
first non-official and self-supporting newspaper was launched
(1860) by a young man named Shinassi, with the support
of his friend Aghah Effendi.   It was called *Terjumani-
Ahval* (Interpreter of Conditions).[1]   This was the first instance of the uniting of an idealist with a capitalist for the
purpose of publishing a paper which was to be the personal
organ of the former, a method which often had to be resorted to in the period of the rise of the Turkish press.   The
capitalists have been in most cases Armenians or Greeks.

The publication of this newspaper marks an epoch in the
history of both Ottoman literature and of the Ottoman language.   Not only was it the first non-official journal in Turkey,
it was the first utterance of the Modern School, that school
which was destined, in the brief space of twenty years, to
sweep from the stage the crumbling débris of five centuries of
Asiaticism [2]

Shinassi (1827-1871), the founder of the paper, was unlike most of the Turkish reformers.   He had studied in
Paris at the expense of the government, and there he had
had excellent opportunities and connections to keep him in
contact with the best French thinkers of the time.   His
line of study was pure science   Upon his return, he

[1] Munif Pasha, *Mejmou'a-i-Funoon* (Constantinople, 1860), vol. i,
no. 1.

[2] Gibb, *History of Ottoman Poetry*, vol. iv, p. 26.

clearly saw what the country required for modernizing
itself. It needed above all, he thought, a new language, a
simple and common means of expression, instead of constant political agitation. He, therefore, set to work to
improve and modernize the language. As a scholar and a
practical man of clear vision he can hardly be understood in
terms of that troublesome time.

His connection with *Terjumani-Ahval* lasted only six
months. Then he parted with his associate Aghah Effendi and established a new paper of his own. This was
Tasviri-Efkiar (The Tablet of Opinion). In this paper,
as in the former, his aim was to assimilate the intellectual
life of Turkey as closely as might be to that of Western
nations. He tried to keep aloof from political troubles,
devoting his attention mostly to scientific and social matters, and especially to the improvement and simplification
of the language.

In 1862, the young discontents organized themselves for
the first time, as a Young Turkish Party. During the same
year, the great writer and agitator Kemal Bey[1] made his
début in newspaper work by joining the staff of Shinassi.
He immediately became the soul of the whole movement.
Shinassi was often glad to leave the management of his
paper to him and to retire to Paris to do research work in
libraries for the purpose of compiling a dictionary of the
Turkish language.

In 1865, *Mushbir*, another paper, established by the enlightened theologian, Ali Souavi, became the center of
Young Turkish agitation. Ali Souavi, had come to Constantinople during that year as a religious preacher. He

[1] Kemal Bey was born in 1831 at Constantinople of Albanian parents (1840)
and died in 1887. As a journalist, novelist, dramatist and political
agitator, he played a prominent part in the movement for Turkey's
regeneration

caused a sensation by his bold sermons. Soon, he saw fit
to create a more general platform for himself by publishing his *Mushbir* (Herald of Glad Tidings). This paper
at once indulged in revolutionary publications and in fierce
attacks against the persons of Aali and Fouad Pasha, the
two leading statesmen of the day.

For the first time the necessity was felt to put some kind
of restraint upon the press The press law of January,
1865, was promulgated and a press bureau instituted to
watch over the execution of law

The law soon proved helpless in checking the revolutionary publications and the personal attacks against those
in power. Then, a step was taken, which has been characteristic of the Turkish system of government ever since.
The government decided, " on account of considerations
of public order, to act, as often as the interests of the country required, through administrative channels, and independently of the existing press law, against newspapers
which should disregard the principles, the observation of
which is the essential condition of a national press."

This regulation suspended the more or less liberal press
law, and opened the way to arbitrary measures. The three
stages followed were warning, suspension, and suppression
of undesirable papers. This practice of promulgating a
liberal law, and suspending it through extraordinary measures became after that time the usual procedure in Turkey.

In 1867, *Mushbir*, the Young Turkish revolutionary organ, became a victim of the new regulation. In the midst
of internal and external troubles, the agitation of the
Young Turks had become more than unwelcome to the
government. An especially frenetic article written on the
occasion of the evacuation of Belgrade was used as a pretext to suppress their organ, and to exile them from the
capital, by appointing them to provincial positions. They

preferred, however, to flee to London, and manage from there, their political agitation. They co-ordinated their *Mushbir* with a Young Turkish paper of minor importance, called *Hurriet* (Liberty), established there in 1864.[1] Also a review named *Oulloum* (Sciences) was published for some time. Besides all this, they kept producing pamphlets of every kind, some of them forming very interesting and precious documents in Turkish literature.

Thousands of copies were regularly sent to Turkey and diffused even in the most remote parts of the country. In spite of the diligence of the police not a single copy fell into the hands of the authorities. In order to understand how this was possible, it must be remembered that Turkey possessed, outside of her own post system, a whole set of foreign postoffices, which she could not control or influence in any way. These postoffices originated, as did all of the privileges conceded by Turkey to the foreign powers, as a specific mark of courtesy. More and more, these privileges took the form of an established right.

Through the treaty of Kutchuk-Kainarji (1774), Russia had obtained permission to have her embassy's mail carried by special messengers. The other embassies promptly followed her in this practice. Little by little the privilege was extended to private correspondence, and finally foreign postoffices were established in the principal cities. What an important part they were destined to play in the intellectual and political life of Turkey will be indicated in the next chapter.

The Young Turkish propaganda was certainly of deep influence in awakening the people and creating a new national consciousness, but politically it was rather destructive.

[1] Vambery, *Deutsche Rundschau*, October, 1893.

It was directed against a circle of able statesmen with political experience and the best of intentions for the welfare of the country.   Their task was hard enough even without this agitation.   On the one hand they had to cope with, and to check, the caprices of Sultan Abdul-Aziz; on the other they had to fight against the intrigues of certain powers, especially Russia, and at the same time to attempt to regenerate, in spite of these intrigues, in spite of the inertia of many sections of the native population, in spite of endless material difficulties, a country in anarchy, in ignorance, and with but a primitive economic equipment. In addition to all this, it was unfortunate to have to be embarrassed by the deadly criticism of the enlightened class. As in the later periods of the Turkish reform movement, radical agitation was more attractive for some of the idealists and patriots than constructive work within the field of practical possibilities.   It is remarkable that the most sweeping reforms in public instruction were realized during the time, when the government was free from the immediate attacks of Young Turkish papers   Between 1867 and 1870, several institutions for higher learning were established, and a system of public education was organized with the aid of French experts.   French became part of the regular curriculum of public schools, and in the most important of them, the Galata-Saray School, it was the language of instruction.   The period was in every respect a French one, and was distinguished, much to the alarm and displeasure of Russia, by intense reform activity Russia resorted to every possible means to check the course of progress in Turkey, so actively, that Fouad Pasha, the leader of the reforms, remarked: " Whenever I lose my way, I find the right way by doing what Russia is hostile to "

The misfortune of France in the War of 1870-71 was a grave blow to Turkey.   The French prestige in the Orient was destroyed. A strong reaction was immediately noticed against reform under French guidance. Shocked by these events, A'ali Pasha, the last great statesman of the old school, died in 1871. His power and influence had constituted an effective check to the follies of the palace and to the intrigues of Russia, as well as to the aspirations of the reactionary factions of the population. At his death, all of these factors triumphed. Mahmoud Nedim Pasha, an ignorant man, was appointed Grand Vezir and soon was nicknamed by the people, *Mahmoudoff*, on account of his being a mere tool of General Ignatieff, the Russian ambassador. Under the intrigues and encouragement of the representative of Russia, a rule of abuse and corruption began which ended in the bankruptcy of the State.

The new government had summoned the Young Turks back from London and Paris, because it felt helpless to deal with the critical situation. They came, but only to become bitter opponents of the corrupt system. The easy life at the Court and the endless abuses very soon stirred up opposition, and forced the enlightened elements to unite, in a common struggle for change and betterment.

Without such conditions to be attacked, the rapid progress in the Turkish press and literature between the years 1871 and 1876 could hardly have been expected to take place, for the reason that there was so little like-mindedness among those interested in the regeneration of the country. Only strong pressure could keep them together or prevent them from rivaling each other.

Kemal Bey, the leading writer of the time, immediately established a paper of his own on his return from London Its name was *Ibret* (Admonition). In its relative influence and effect, this paper has hardly been surpassed by any other periodical in Modern Turkey. Other papers followed, but very few had a lasting life, and very few were, to any extent, a financial success   In a country where a very small number of people besides the state officials could read and write, the achievements of the press could hardly be expressed in large numbers. Still, again and again, there were enterprises undertaken on the part of young men with capital and some writing ability to issue a paper and bring home to the people at large, the meaning of right, of duty, of patriotism and private initiative   Their failure did not deter other young men from trying the experiment for themselves. Besides the voluntary disappearances from the scene, it was an every-day occurrence for papers to be suspended or suppressed by the government.

The journalists of prominence were often sent away from the capital by being appointed to provincial offices   Among them, Kemal Bey, the editor of the *Ibret*, whose paper had been repeatedly suspended, was appointed Governor of Galippoli.   He resigned, however, after a few months and resumed the publication of the *Ibret*   In 1875, the popular enthusiasm created by the performance of his play *Vatan* (Fatherland), in which a Turkish girl of seventeen was represented as disguising herself as a man, and becoming a soldier, like her fiancé, in a campaign against Russia, caused the government to exile the whole company of popular writers to the Island of Cyprus   In addition to these measures a stamp duty of one-fifth of a cent per copy was imposed on all political publications.

In spite of the repressive policy of the government the press continued to grow, both in numbers and in quality. In 1860, the whole empire possessed but one official and one semi-official weekly, both supported by the government. In 1872,[1] there were three dailies, two papers appearing three times a week, a satirical semi-weekly, a satirical

---

[1] *The official almanac (Salnamé) for the year 1872*, chapter on the press.

weekly, a weekly police gazette, a military weekly, and a commercial weekly. The publications in non-Turkish languages were as follows: French, six dailies (*Levant Herald, Levant Times*—these partly in English, *Phare du Bosphore, Esprit, La Turquie, Courrier d'Orient*) and a weekly; Armenian, three dailies, two semi-weeklies, and six weeklies; Greek, one daily, two appearing three times a week, three semi-weeklies, one bi-weekly; Bulgarian, three weeklies and a monthly; Hebrew, one weekly. One of the Armenian papers was the *Avedepar*, published since 1853 by the American Mission Board. It is still published and has a circulation amounting to several thousands. There is no paper in Turkey to compete with it in length and continuity of existence. It is a sort of a family weekly, giving mostly cultural news. It also has a Greek Edition and a Turkish Edition in Armenian characters The Board has no periodical publication in Turkish, but it has published many Turkish works, such as dictionaries and textbooks.

In 1876, there were forty-seven papers published in Constantinople.[1] Thirteen were in Turkish, seven of them being dailies, two semi-weeklies, one a political weekly, one a satirical weekly, one a medical monthly and one an illustrated monthly. The papers in non-Turkish languages included nine in Greek, nine in Armenian, seven in French, three in Bulgarian, two in English, two in Hebrew, one in German, and one in Arabic. These forty-seven papers published in 1876 do not represent the maximum number attained between 1871 and 1876. The stamp duty and other difficulties had already caused a selection to take place, from which only those well founded in the way of means and equipment survived. Before that the number had been

---

[1] Ubicini et Courteille, *Etat Présent de l'Empire Ottoman* (Paris, 1876), pp. 167 *et seq.*

an exceedingly shifting one. At times, there were four or five illustrated Turkish satirical weeklies. Courteille and Ubicini, who published their work on " The present State of the Ottoman Empire " in 1876, and consulted the official almanac of 1876 for information regarding the press, found that some of the papers mentioned there did not exist any more, while there were several new ones, not included in the official text.

— The activity of the press was not wholly confined to Constantinople. After the promulgation of the provincial administration law of 1864, there began to be established official weeklies, at the seat of every province. They were published in Turkish and often also in the language of the dominating local non-Turkish community. The first was the *Tona* (Danube), published in the Danubia Province (Bulgaria) in Turkish and Bulgarian. As a class these publications were of limited importance. Very rarely, excepting when an especially active official happened to take charge of one, did any provincial paper, in one place or another, show any signs of life. The *Ibret* of Constantinople in its issue of June 19, 1872, makes an ironical review of the last numbers of the provincial papers received from different parts of the empire, and finds in them, besides official communications, only bits of news regarding malformed specimens of new breed among the cattle of some individuals in the community. At times there were attempts made by people in exile or educated natives to publish non-official papers in provincial towns, but they were of no consequence and duration Constantinople remained the sole intellectual center in the empire and its great influence and authority prevented the provinces from developing a local intellectual life of their own.

Together with the numerical growth of the press in Constantinople, came refinement and specialization in the methods of influencing and educating the public. The stage began to be used for creating patriotic emotions and the novel for preparing a new social order. The hero of the new novels was often a Young Turk, thirsting for Western civilization, without becoming weak in his religious feelings and moral ideals, while the opponent was either a reactionary old Turk, or a young man degenerated through contact with Western life.

Ahmed Midhat Effendi was the name of the remarkable man who let others fight for political ideas and devoted his whole attention to the treatment of social problems, writing a great many novels and short stories on these lines. The marriage customs and the position of women were the points he kept especially in mind in his struggle for a sound social system. At the same time, he published two periodicals, called *Kirk-Anbar* (Forty Stores),[1] and *Tagardjik* (The Wallet), which tried to acquaint the Turkish reader with every branch of Western knowledge. In a single number of *Kirk-Anbar*, there could be found essays on the chemical composition of the egg, on the poetry of Schiller, on metaphysics, on the philosophy of history, on mesmerism

Ahmed Midhat Effendi was, however, not the pioneer in the work of popularizing knowledge, as he was in some other branches. There was already a scientific magazine, named *Mejmou'a-i-Funoun* (Scientific Magazine), established in 1279 A. H. (1861) by Munif Pasha, who later became minister of public instruction, and whose career is closely connected with the history of modern education in Turkey. This magazine had many of the ministers and high dignitaries for contributors and was the organ of the

---

[1] The term is used in Turkish for a man acquainted with every branch of knowledge.

society for popularizing knowledge.[1]   It was published un-
interruptedly for four years, then suspended, because most
members of the society were government officials who rapidly advanced in their career and became unable to devote
much attention and time to outside matters, and was re-established in 1882 by Munif Pasha, its original founder.   Its
example was so stimulating that, within seven months after
its foundation in 1861, two new periodicals of the same type
sprang up, the *Ibr-u-Intibah* and the *Mir'att*.   Most of the
popular periodicals which followed these three had very
short lives but there were some that existed for a year or
more, like *Hadika* (The Orchard)   To form an idea about
this type of publication, it might be of use to give an outline
of the contents of one or two numbers of this weekly.   The
number of May 27, 1870, of *Hadika* begins with an article
of thanks to a notable of the City of Monastir, who do-
nated yearly subscriptions of the weekly to the schools of
his city   Next comes an appeal to the young men to acquire an earnest scientific training and to devote their energies to productive branches of work.   After this follows an
imaginary conversation with an ignorant man of the old
type about the education of his children   Next in order
are articles in a popular style and partly in dialogue form
on astronomy, photography, botany, agriculture, the historical development of steam engines, the process of steel
manufacturing, the future of our planet, and a serial on the
" history of philosophers."

[1] This society displayed great activity between 1861 and 1863 in
educating the masses. For this purpose, the magazine in question and
popular text-books were published, a public reading room established,
and popular courses given in natural sciences and history The courses
were open to everybody and had an attendance varying between 300
and 500. According to the information obtained from the files of the
Mejmou'a-i-Funoon, the society also patronized a national exhibition
of agricultural and manufactured articles and agitated in different ways
to bring about private and collective economic undertakings.

The number of October 29, 1870 contains articles on botany, the lunar calendar, mathematics, metaphysics, breeding of domestic animals, lithography, the evolution of languages, the measures to be taken against careless druggists, a critical study of the methods followed in Turkish elementary schools, a dialogue advocating co-operative economic enterprises among Turks, and a serial publication of the biography of the theologian Rufinus. Many of the articles were translations from French, bringing a large part of the reading public for the first time in touch with occidental knowledge. Many were undoubtedly shocked by the new ways of explaining the nature and relation of things offered to them.

Deeper and more general was the feeling of shock in the Turkish mind of that time, however, against the methods of satirical publications. It was not easy for the dignified and reverent Turk of two generations ago to become used to a satirical treatment of serious matters. Still, supported by an enterprising Armenian capitalist, they could maintain their ground and acquire more and more influence. Between 1871 and 1876, there were at times four or five satirical weeklies and semi-weeklies, *Hayal* (Phantasy) *Djingrakli-Tatar* (Courrier with Bells), and *Diogenes*, being the most prominent. They were ably edited, and could make with their indirect allusions, a more effective opposition against the abuses of the government than the political papers Like these satirical papers, most of the political papers were also mainly tools at the hands of men with advanced ideas for shaping public opinion. They represented the tendencies among the minority, but hardly the response of the majority to the course of change taking place in different branches of the Turkish life. The main reason for this consisted in the fact that the religious fanatics, averse to change, had not the means and the necessary training for publishing papers. They could not even use the pulpit for checking the process of modernization. Sultan Abdul Aziz did not permit religion to be made a pretext for interfering with his or other people's behavior He offered a unique spectacle of an absolute and misruling Sultan in Turkey, who did not use religious fanaticism to consolidate his position against the opposing radical elements and who did not take any notice of religious prejudice. The result was twofold. the fanatical elements forgot the Young Turks and their dislike for them, and concentrated their attention against the person of the Sultan and the easy life at his palace. The Young Turkish writers thus found opportunity to deal freely with social problems and advocate the changes that they saw necessary On the other hand, the common hostility against the Sultan, although emanating from unlike sources, brought the fanatics to the point of allying themselves with the Young Turks for the purpose of common action. In 1876, when Sultan Abdul Aziz was dethroned, the most radical Young Turks and the most fanatical theological students alike had a share in the conspiracy

·The only attempt to expound the views of the old Turks, was made by the daily *Bassirett* (Watchfulness) For some time, the *Bassirett* had a reactionary policy, concealing rather than exposing the existing evils But the atmosphere was so full of militancy, that it could not resist the trend of the times very long. More and more, it began to draw attention to the achievements of Western nations and to the shortcomings at home, but it still remained conservative in tone, and displayed outbursts of fanaticism and ignorance on many occasions. It had the largest circulation among the papers of the time, and was financially a success. It is remarkable that the popular tradition claims for it a circulation of thirty thousand. There is not the slightest possibility that a Turkish daily published before 1876 had even one-third of that circulation, but, in later years, under Abdul Hamid's government, the press was so much oppressed that the people were naturally inclined to look back to former times through a magnifying glass.

It must be remembered, however, that a circulation of a few thousands had in that period, when the old Turkish social life had not quite begun to disintegrate, a greater importance than a much larger circulation to-day. A single copy could reach a great many more people through the medium of the coffee house and through the evening gatherings of neighbors in the different houses of the neighborhood. Besides, most of the readers carefully kept and collected one or more papers. As only a select class could read and write, the readers were also relatively intelligent and appreciative. When *Istikbal* (The Future), one of the dailies, published in its number of June 24, 1876, an article of thanks and praise for Sir Henry Elliot, the British Ambassador, generally known in Turkey as a warm friend of the Turks, and as a believer in Turkey's national future, the regular supply of the paper was soon exhausted, and the article had to be published again and again, " in order to give every son of the fatherland opportunity to acquire a copy of it."

Up until 1876, the uniform price of papers was one piaster (four cents) per copy, and from ten to fifteen dollars for yearly subscriptions. Most of the papers after 1871, owned their printing presses.

The journalists as a class were distinguished more by their wild night-life than by anything else. They considered themselves justified in drinking to excess, as they had to fulfill a delicate task, and were every moment exposed to the danger of exile or prison. They were also poorly paid. Still the calling was very attractive to adventurous natures and many were glad to volunteer their services, without expecting any pay in return. What is more, the *Hadika* (1870) announced in all its issues, that manuscripts on science and art sent in by people of education might be published gratuitously.

The main feature of the papers was the editorial article News, for its own sake was not published unless it concerned the public life in its most general aspect or the political conditions and diplomatic relations of other countries. Provincial and city news items were published only when they could be used for a warning or a moral hint. There was a great difference, however, between the paper of 1870 and 1876 in this regard. The course of development led to the concentration of attention from far-off countries and conditions to the more and more immediate environment. With occasional exceptions, the advertisements related to new books.

Going through the copies of the papers of this period, one cannot help being impressed by the general anxiety for survival as a nation. This was expressed in regard to matters of external safety, as well as with reference to problems like decreasing population and infanticide. The *Istikbal* had this motto: ' The body of the Fatherland is a united whole Under no pretext can it be divided '' The *Bassirett*, in 1875, made a vigorous campaign regarding the decrease of population, under the headline, '' The Nation is Becoming Wrecked.'' It pointed out that owing to the military service, to the lack of hygienic knowledge, and to the spread of infanticide the population was decreasing with tremendous rapidity, and whole villages were disappearing one after the other in the region inhabited by the Turkish element. This problem of population was dealt with from time to time by all papers, and the government was urged to take speedy action. Contrary to the prevailing idea of former times, when almost the entire Turkish population was confident of its superiority over all others and attributed its misfortune to fate or heavenly punishment, the press spurred by imminent dangers, spoke again and again of the national inferiority in economic enterprise, in education, in habits, in organization.

The change was a tremendous one. Owing mainly to the press, in the last instance, the sleeping, self-satisfied mediaeval community had become within two or three decades a self-conscious, self-critical and potentially progressive one.)The old written language which served for creating ornamental phrases and forms, but not for expressing simple ideas, gave way to a practical medium for expressing thought; the old individualistic struggle of the preceding period for self-interest was superseded by public spirit.

The day came, when, inflamed by the suicidal policy of the government, the public felt strong enough to assert its will and to demand through imposing street demonstrations, the removal from office of all corrupt officials Sultan Abdul Aziz was a weak man and open to every kind of suggestion. He yielded without resistance, but this surrender did not save his throne as he hoped. The first act of the new government was to obtain a *fatva*[1] from the Sheikh-ul-Islam, Hairroullah Effendi to dethrone him on a charge of misrule.

Every obstacle that had stood in the way of a good and honest government, and of the application of reforms seemed now to have been removed. A new era seemed to have dawned suddenly, and Young Turkey believed that she had finally triumphed.

It is of interest to note that the conservative *Bassiret*

---

[1] The word explained on page 23.

went further than the other papers in celebrating the event. A few hours after the dethronement a gratuitous number of the *Bassirett* was distributed in the streets of Constantinople. It announced in frenetic terms that " the nation had at last got rid of the despot and of General Ignatieff ". The Russian ambassador who had only a few days previously, caused the *Levant Herald* to be persecuted for a disrespectful allusion to his person, refrained from taking steps against the *Bassirett*.

The new Sultan, Mourad V, possessed a very good and kind disposition. Having been kept in seclusion as a Prince by Abdul Aziz, his uncle, he had used his time to advantage in learning French and in acquiring Western knowledge. Under his rule, the Young Turks had perfect control of the situation. All the exiled journalists were recalled, and the press began a new and unchecked activity. The government was occupied in drafting a liberal constitution, and in dealing with the grave internal troubles and the danger of intervention.

Meanwhile, an event took place, which proved of fatal consequence in more than one way. A few days after the dethronement, the deposed Sultan was found dead in his room. In all probability he had ended his own life, but it was pretended for political purposes, that he had been murdered The new Sultan was so deeply shocked by the tragic death of his uncle, that he soon began to show signs of mental disorder. Only three months after his accession another *fatva* dethroned him on the ground of insanity.

Before taking this step, the leaders of the reform party had obtained from the Prince Abdul Hamid, the next heir to the throne, specific pledges as to his future rule. The Prince appeared to be even more liberal than the Young Turks themselves, and promised more than he was asked for. Among other things, he pledged himself to proclaim immediately a constitution, to appoint two of the most advanced young Turkish journalists his secretaries and to choose only Young Turks for high positions in the palace.   Upon this basis he was allowed to ascend the throne, on September 1, 1876, as Sultan Abdul Hamid II, to the terror and disappointment of nearly every section of the population. Abdul Hamid was unpopular to the same extent as his brother was beloved.   Even those papers which were always on the side of authority and the ruling government, abstained from welcoming the new sovereign.   On the day of his accession to the throne, they merely gave expression to their sorrow for the fate of Sultan Mourad.   In order to quiet the public mind, the semi-official *Djeridé-i-Havadis* pointed out that Sultan Abdul Hamid had lived for long years in the same palace with Sultan Mourad, and that he was very likely to have been influenced by his brother's good character and broad knowledge.   The only guarantee the people had that the unpopular man would not turn out to be a dangerous despot consisted of his pledges.   The Young Turks were not long in finding out for themselves, that pledges did not mean much, when a strong Sultan did not intend to keep them.

CHAPTER IV

THE HAMIDIAN PERIOD

THE history of Turkey between 1876 and 1908 is, in every respect a *Hamidian* one. Every branch of life and of activity in that period was, in some way or other, influenced by the strong will and evil genius of a single man · Sultan Abdul Hamid   For him, there existed but one consideration and that was the absolute maintenance of his safety and personal power.   Outside of that, everything in his eyes was an exciting game which he took delight in playing against a large number of adversaries, mostly patriots and idealists, who were by far inferior to him in cunning.   Every trick, every seeming compromise, he allowed to himself in the game, the point was to win, to win by all means.

When he ascended the throne, he found himself entirely set aside by those whom he considered secretly his enemies in the coming contest.   The Young Turks, self-confident through the easy dethronement of two Sultans within three months, considered him a mere tool in their hands.   The press felt itself above him and gave over-emphasis to this feeling of superiority.   The *Vakit* (Time) stated on every occasion that the real sovereignity rested with the people and that they could depose their Sultan whenever they chose to do so.   The *Istikbal* (Future) reminded the people again and again that the constitution was not a gift of the sovereign, but was obtained by a group of patriots after a hard struggle.   The *Ittihad* (Unity) pointed out in its number of November 1, 1879, that the people could no longer be

52   [52

satisfied by paper measures, that practical activity ought to
begin at last to strengthen the sovereign rights of the people.
Zia Bey, one of the most influential journalists and the one
most dreaded by the Sultan, said, addressing an audience
of secondary school students, that a Sultan was " only the
chief servant of the people."

The response of a strong, ambitious and evil-intentioned
man like Abdul Hamid to such a situation could not but be
an attitude of bitter hostility, and a desperate struggle for
power.   He was too clever, however, to take any rash steps.

He clearly saw that to appoint Young Turks as palace
secretaries and dignitaries as he had pledged himself to do,
would curb every possibility of rising to absolute power.
He, accordingly, broke his word and formed a palace
camarilla from the most noted reactionaries.

He understood perfectly, that absolute power could not
go hand in hand with a free and vigorously edited press,
such as the one the new era had suddenly produced.   The
Young Turkish press had, in fact, thrown the few conservative papers out of the field and had worked wonders
among the people within a few months.   It had given the
readers a new sort of national enthusiasm, it had taught
them that they had rights which arbitrary sovereigns had
withheld from them, and that a democratic constitution
based upon the idea of the rights of all Ottomans without
distinction of race and creed would immediately cure and
reform everything.   Many of the religious dignitaries and
theological students were believers in this panacea, and had
become strong supporters of Midhat Pasha, the great statesman and national leader   The leading journalist Zia Bey
was almost worshiped by the whole capital.

The Sultan was more than alarmed by this state of affairs.   He always read the papers with great care, and
often sent extracts of articles that he was not pleased with,

to the Sublime Porte, dictating the action to be taken against those concerned   The correspondence between the palace and the Grand-Vezir Midhat Pasha, published by Ali Haidar Midhat Bey [1] throws a great deal of light on the dread Abdul Hamid entertained for the press.   All his communications ended with phrases such as : " His majesty considers it urgent to find means to put an end to such doings in the press," or " If such acts are tolerated, the papers will not fail to profit by the license, and abuse it   His Majesty orders that the imperial commands issued against certain of the papers shall be executed as soon as possible by way of example."

Midhat Pasha, the Grand-Vezir, being an ardent supporter of a free press, Abdul Hamid was not long in coming to the conclusion that decisive steps had to be taken in doing away with the Young Turkish supremacy. before it acquired an unassailable position.   On the one hand, he tried to prevent the publication of telegrams from the provinces expressing enthusiasm regarding the impending proclamation of the constitution; on the other hand, he began to apply his skillful tactics to oust the leaders   The new spirit in Turkey had no natural foundation   It was only upheld by influential and enlightened leaders, supported by the pressure of circumstances.   With these leaders eliminated and the press subdued, the country which was under a cross fire from external dangers and internal unrest and dissatisfaction, could become an easy prey to an absolute ruler.   Besides, the plans of the Young Turks to separate the secular and religious powers, and to create a new and neutral national type of " Ottoman ", who should have equal rights of citizenship without distinction of race or color or creed, had produced a great deal of irritation among some

[1] *Life of Midhat Pasha* (London, 1903), pp. 122-127.

sections of the population. The *Bassirett*, to some extent, gave utterance to their feelings. Some of the people attempted to cause agitation by preaching and by distributing secret literature.

The popular journalist, Zia Bey [1] was the first man to be removed. According to the policy, applied as far as possible by the Sultan against his political opponents, he was invested with the highest honors and titles. As the population of Constantinople attempted to keep their favorite among themselves by electing him for deputy, he was hastily removed from Constantinople as the General Governor of Syria.

In the meantime, the dream cherished for decades by the Young Turks seemed to have been realized. On December 23, 1876, a liberal constitution was proclaimed with great pomp, to the general delight of most of the elements of the population, and to the stupefaction of the international conference, sitting at Constantinople to decide the future status of some parts of European Turkey.

The enthusiasm and surprise were not to last very long, however. On February 4, 1877, Midhat Pasha, the father of the constitutional movement, was taken from his house without any previous notice and escorted on board the imperial yacht *Izziddin* to be carried away from Turkey to some European port. Up to the last moment, the

---

[1] Zia Bey was born in Constantinople in 1829, the son of a clerk of the Galata Custom House. He had a brilliant career as a journalist, poet, educator and political agitator. He died in 1880 in Adana, sick and broken-hearted at what he deemed the failure of his life-work. The degree of his disappointment is expressed in the following utterance, translated into English by Mr. Gibb (*History of Ottoman Poetry*, vol. v, p. 69) :

" Naught but sorrows, on the loyal to this Empire ever wait;
  Sheerest madness is devotion to this People and this State."

Sultan was not sure that he might so easily rid himself of the popular leader. The captain of the yacht was ordered to halt near Constantinople for a day, and bring Midhat Pasha back immediately in the event of a popular outbreak.

The blow was so sudden that everybody was taken by surprise, and no concerted action could take place in the city guarded by military force.

Then came the war of 1877-78 with Russia The situation caused by the war, was of course, a great advantage to the purpose and policy of Abdul Hamid The attention of the people and the press was centered on external danger. The Young Turkish press itself, unaware of the approaching peril, had frequently advocated the war. In the excitement of patriotism, all the noble watchwords of the French Revolution were forgotten. The dissolution of the Parliament by the Sultan attracted little attention. Midhat Pasha, in London, had to be a helpless spectator of the crumbling of his life-work, had to see how Russia, after having crippled Turkey internally by secret intrigues, tried openly to administer to her a final and fatal blow.

During the progress of the war, all the foundations were laid for the despotic system which was to dominate Turkey for several decades. The palace and the Sultan became the center of all public activity. Even the operations of the campaign were directed by the Sultan himself, a fact which explains why Turkey was so badly beaten after having been so successful in the beginning. His desire to attend personally to every detail of governmental business [1] was the main concern of his life, after his anxiety for the safety of his throne.

The press had a special place in the Sultan's daily ac-

---

[1] Gabriel Charmes, *L'Avenir de La Turque*, Paris, 1883, gives an interesting and almost prophetic account of the life and of the future designs of the Sultan.

tivity.   He read all the papers and took immediate action
where he deemed it necessary.   He kept on banishing the
incorrigible idealists, some others he bought with money,
titles and honors, and he appealed to the religious and
patriotic feelings of the fanatical and unenlightened ones.
As a result, the militant and vigorous press was reduced
within one year to a ready tool at the Sultan's hands.   The
stamp duty was continued as a general measure, making it
almost impossible for independent papers to exist, while the
papers proving their submission and devotion were richly
subventioned and rewarded.

~ By 1877, many of the papers had two different styles of
language.   The one was the new Turkish, simplified by the
Young Turkish writers.   It was used in relation to everything but matters regarding the person or the government
of the Sultan.   For such purposes the old forms and pompous phrases were used   These were taken both by the
writer and the reader as matters of mere formality.   The
way in which the *Mussavat* (Equality) of August 11, 1877
announced the news that the Sultan had ordered one of his
private yachts to be equipped with cannon, and used as an
auxiliary warship, may serve here as an illustration :

His imperial Majesty, whose person abounds in sacred qualities and whose chief imperial desires are directed to the end of
raising the necessaries of war to the most supreme degree of
perfection in order to safeguard the sacred rights of His Sublime Empire, has made to the many acts and efforts, he, as our
great and sublime benefactor, has been putting forth since the
beginning of the present war, for bringing the military equipment up to a degree satisfactory to his august mind, one more
addition, in deigning to issue an imperial order (the orders of
the august holder of the Crown are always full of kindness
and generosity) to the effect that the imperial yacht, called
" Stamboul ", which is in the personal service of our august

Majesty, whose person abounds in lofty qualities, should be equipped with cannon and be added to the imperial navy. Measures to this effect have been taken accordingly.

During the war, the contents of the papers mainly consisted of official communications concerning the military situation, of translations from foreign papers regarding the diplomatic situation, and of occasional articles. These articles dealt mostly with the refutation of certain publications in the Russian press, or with patriotic appeals to the people in connection with the war. The main motive which found expression in such appeals was the desire for recognition by the Western world. "Europe is looking at us. The Ottomans must show their traditional patriotism and bravery," was the usual conclusion of patriotic articles. The papers were very sensitive regarding atrocity charges, and they showed great zeal in refuting such allegations, and in condemning the Russians on the same score. The indifferent attitude of European powers, particularly England, was often criticized. The *Mussavat* (Equality), stated in its number of August 13, 1877, that "Europe by its indifferent attitude had blackened the pages of the history of humanity and civilization and it was for the Ottomans to clean and glorify those pages again by driving back, single-handed, the invading enemy."

The spirit of awakening and self-consciousness of the press of a few years previous had thus given way to a naïve self-deception. This was more markedly shown later in connection with the Tunisian question. The *Vakit* (Time), criticizing the decision of the government in sending a fleet to Tunisian waters to remonstrate against the French occupation said: "This is hardly necessary, the despatch of a single row-boat would be enough to arouse the population of North Africa and to have the French army thrown back into the sea." As a consequence, the people lost interest in the papers, the old prestige of the press vanished, until the papers themselves became aware of their inefficiency.

In August 1877, the *Terjuman-i-Efkiar* (Interpreter of Ideas), a paper printed in Armenian characters and in the Turkish language, published an article pointing out that the Turkish press had no prestige abroad, and no influence among its readers, that it was ridiculed by the press of other countries, never being taken seriously or quoted by them. The conclusion stated that the Ottoman press deserved such treatment, as it had no intrinsic value, and that it would have to raise its quality in order to become more effective This article was quoted by all the papers, and all of them sadly acknowledged that the statements were correct. The *Umran* (Upheaval) which began to be published on August 31, 1877, contains in its fourth number, a letter from a reader who expresses his dissatisfaction at the state of the press, reminding the journalists " that the press cannot only cause the progress of a country, as often stated, but can also bring about its ruin and destruction, if managed by short-sighted and favor-seeking men."

After the war, many of the papers were in great financial distress. Several of them had to suspend their publication. The "*Osmanli*" which attempted to transform itself into a satirical publication was notified by the government, that publications of that type could no longer be tolerated. Repeated attempts were made to induce the government to abolish the stamp tax, but they were not of any avail.

After having subdued the press and become master of the whole situation, the main concern of Abdul Hamid, was the existence of Midhat Pasha, the great liberal leader. During his sojourn in Europe, Midhat had received so much attention and esteem from people and governments alike, that Abdul Hamid felt it to be dangerous to permit his most dreaded opponent to live outside the sphere of his influence. In 1879, he was appointed Governor of Syria, and later Governor of Smyrna. His persecution had only increased his popularity everywhere. His very existence became a danger in the eyes of the Sultan Repeated attempts to murder and poison him having failed, he was openly accused of having taken part in the " murder " of the deposed Sultan Abdul Aziz, who, according to all evidence, had committed suicide. He was condemned to death after a sham trial in 1881. Thanks to the intervention of the British ambassador, the death sentence was changed into one of life imprisonment in Taif, Arabia. He was sent there with a large number of other statesmen and liberals, where he and one of his companions were strangled in 1883. Zia Pasha, the famous journalist, had previously died in 1880 in Adana, not being able to survive for any length of time the failure of his work. Kemal Bey, the great writer who had also been kept away from Constantinople as Governor of Mitylene and Gallipoli, followed him in 1887. A group of journalists and enlightened young men of other professions, perished while making a desperate attempt under the leadership of the popular journalist Ali Souavi, to free and restore the deposed Sultan Mourad V. This took place in 1878 after the Treaty of San Stefano was concluded, and agitation was being made by England for the assembly of the Congress of Berlin. According to Yorga [1] the Young Turkish agitation was one of the reasons which induced Russia to agree to the idea of a revisionary congress.

The Young Turkish downfall meant the final defeat of the idea of secularizing the state and of unifying all the citizens upon a national basis as Ottomans. It meant the end of an open struggle for betterment. To what extent

---

[1] Yorga, *Geschichte des Osmanischen Reiches,* vol v, p. 591.

this struggle would have been successful, had it not been
opposed by a strong man like Abdul Hamid can hardly
be surmised.   Midhat Pasha's rapid and marvelous—success in the most disturbed of Provinces, to which he went
as Governor, proved that a strong, resourceful and honest
leader could work wonders in Turkey.   The increase of
Ottoman patriotism among the non-Turks and the changing
attitude among the Turks themselves showed that systematic
effort could within a comparatively short time, at least for
the purposes of practical politics, substitute for the group
based upon blood or religious relationship, a social system
based upon civic principles   The population could be
moulded.   There was no half-educated turbulent element to
interfere seriously with the activity of the leaders.   They
were far above the group type and had come in contact with
the scientific spirit and energy of the industrial countries
of the West, while the great mass of the population lived in
isolation and had to depend upon the accepted knowledge
and economic equipment of the middle ages for their mental
and material existence.   On the other hand, those who
know the character and extent of Russian secret intrigues
and open policy, may rightly doubt whether Turkey would
have been able to progress in a normal way, even if a personality like Abdul Hamid had not appeared on the stage of
of her history, and other conditions besides had been favorable.   It may even be argued that the personality and system
of Abdul Hamid were to a great extent of Russian creation.
Not only was the Sultan guided by Russian example, but the
threatening atmosphere of external dangers resulting from
the Russian policy also backed him in his despotic moves

   The policy of the Sultan was not to save and cure through
an open struggle as the Young Turkish policy was, it was
rather to divide and keep all dangerous elements in opposition to each other with a view to maintain the situation as it

was. ⌐His most formidable weapon was religion.   He resorted to every possible trick to gain prestige as a religious
lord among the fanatical masses and in the Mohammedan
world.   He succeeded, more and more, in arousing the sus-
ceptibilities of the masses against the educated classes, and in
making the ignorant look with contempt upon the educated.
For instance, the dress and manners of women were often
used to arouse fanaticism and to please the fanatics.   The
women had acquired a great deal of liberty under the reign
of the former Sultan.   They had become less careful regarding veiling and more unrestricted in going about as they
chose.   It was very easy to take advantage of this situation to please the masses.   The *Wakit* (Times) of June
12, 1881, published an official announcement regarding the
dress and the public manners of women.   In this it was
stated that " some women were seen in the streets and in
public places dressed in ways contrary to the local customs
and Mohammedan traditions, thereby causing contempt and
hatred among people of honesty, and that His imperial
Majesty, our august lord and Sultan, our great benefactor
to whom our gratitude should have no limits, the sublime
protector of religion and morality and corroborator of manners and customs, was deeply grieved in his imperial heart
about this state of affairs " / The women were then warned
to keep within the ancient limits and to be orderly

In spite of the religious zeal of the Sultan and his building within a few years a form of theocracy without equal in
Turkish history, the religious teachers and theological students as a class were held under more restricted control
than other classes of people.   The Sultan knew perfectly
well that the religion which he was making use of so suc-
cessfully could be used against himself.   Any kind of concerted action among the theological students, the Sultan

most dreaded and tried to prevent by his favor, spy, and secret " elimination " system.

• The more this system was crystallized, the more circumscribed became the position of the press. In the beginning, these restrictions had one advantage; they brought about an atmosphere of artificial quiet in the midst of internal and external troubles, in which attention could be given to literary and scientific matters. The daily papers which were not allowed to deal freely with politics became more and more like magazines. They devoted most of their space to popular articles of a scientific nature, to cultural news from foreign countries, and to fiction. The *Terjuman-i-Hakikat* (Interpreter of Truth) published, in its daily issues, the history of every country in the world, popular treatises on different branches of knowledge, besides a great variety of novels and articles. These, as well as similar serial publications in other papers, were always published in book form. The production of books was not, however, confined to these alone. Books of all varieties appeared in great number. Many of them were translations of exciting French novels, but they were not useless, as they acquainted the reader with an entirely different world, customs and ideas. Besides, books of a serious character were also well represented.[1]

Ebouzzia Tevfik Bey, a close friend and disciple of the great writer Kemal Bey, published under the name of *Ebouzzia's Library* a long list of books, mostly written by Turkish authors. These books were very carefully printed, and were of real value. So also was a fortnightly magazine published by the same man under the title of *Ebouzzia's*

[1] A list of three hundred and three of the works published in 1890 is given in *Journal Asiatique*, section 8, volume 17. This list indicates the extent of intellectual activity and the great variety of the existing interests.

Magazine, which constituted the center of intellectual life in Turkey, as long as it was published.[1]

During the Russian War, and the two years following, there was no direct censorship of the press. The Sultan had so perfect a control of the situation that he could afford to leave to the press its nominal freedom. In 1880, probably on account of the pending trial of Midhat Pasha, a censorship was instituted in the ministry for public instruction. It was not very rigid and did not include a pre-publication examination of the papers. The usual method followed by the censors was to go to newspaper offices and give instructions, in these terms, for instance: " The government has a deal with Germany, during the next few days, and nothing shall be written to offend that power or to weaken the government's position." Measures were generally taken after the publication of the papers to punish offending writers and to restrain the papers from repeating similar offences.

In 1890, a more and more restrictive policy began to be followed regarding the press. The ministry of the interior was charged with the censorship, the ministry of public instruction retaining the right of authorizing the publication of books. The authorities were forbidden to issue permits for the publication of periodicals without the knowledge and express authorization of the Sultan. As the Sultan was averse to giving such authorizations, new papers could appear only under exceptional circumstances

This new attitude was taken, because the Young Turkish

---

[1] *Mejmon'a-i-Funoon* (Constantinople, 1882), ser. ii, no. 1, contains a list of 22 periodicals published in Constantinople at that time, including *Ebouzzia's Magazine* and excluding itself. Most of these periodicals are of a literary and popular character. There is among them a weekly for women, called *Hanimlar* (Women) and published by Araguel, one of the leading booksellers and publishers of the time.

activity seemed to be gaining ground every day. The press
had been able to do propaganda work, in spite of the restrictions imposed. The censors were men of ignorance
who merely took care that forbidden words and terms, like
constitution, oppression, Midhat Pasha, should not be used.
They could not realize that forbidden ideas might be expressed with great advantage in harmless-sounding words
or through indirect allusion. They also could not see any
harm in publications of a general nature which did not touch
upon political questions and aimed only at enlightening the
readers on certain social problems. There were men in the
press who could take advantage of the situation. Especially
Mourad Bey, the leading figure in the press of the time, had
made himself, through his novels, his historical works and
his paper *Mizan* (Balance) the idol of the intellectual
classes. Saïd Bey, another prominent journalist took delight in openly satirizing the person and the government of
Abdul Hamid. Having been the cause of the suppression
of several papers, he could no longer find employment in
the press, so he devoted his time to writing and secretly
diffusing political satires, and in coining slogans for the
Young Turkish agitation. After repeatedly escaping punishment by promising to remain orderly in the future, he
was exiled to Arabia.

The alarming signs of militancy were not confined to the
press and to the secret organizations among students, but,
to the terror of Abdul Hamid, religious preachers in several
mosques began to attack his rule also. In 1891, the religious agitation was particularly strong. As a result, the
preacher of the Kilidj-Ali mosque disappeared from his
pulpit. He was probably exiled by the palace to an un-
known destination.

The papers in Turkey could not, of course, give publicity to such events, unless they received communications

from the palace respecting them, and these would be of such a nature as to misguide the reading public. But there were Young Turkish papers in foreign countries which made it their specialty to give expression to every kind of news and opinion certain to displease Abdul Hamid. Previously, in 1881, an anti-Hamidian paper had been published in Athens by a man named Essad Effendı. In 1891, Mr. Demetrius Georgiades, an Ottoman Greek, established in Parıs a paper called *La Tırquıe Contemporaine*, as an " organ of Young Turkey "; but he had to give up his work by order of the French government.

The real struggle began, however, in 1892 when Ahmed Riza Bey, the director of public ınstruction of the Province of Hudavendıguar, fled to Europe and established his *Meshverett* (Delıberation).

In 1894, the Armenian massacres caused great irritation among the Turkish patrıots   The necessity for urgent action against the Hamıdıan regime was strongly felt, especially by the students. Four medical students laid the foundation of the Secret *Committee of Union and Progress*. This central body soon established branch organizations in different districts of the city, in several ministrıes including the civıl list administration of the Sultan, in all higher governmental schools, both military and civil, and in the private boardıng school " Noumouna-ı-Terakkı " (Sample of Progress). Besides, there were branches in Beyrouth, Damascus and Rhodes. The secret literature distributed and the personal agitation aroused, fell upon very receptive ground

The flight of Mourad Bey, the popular journalıst, to Egypt gave great impetus to the movement. He was charged by the *Committee* to represent ıt abroad and to publish his paper in Egypt, later in Switzerland, as a Committee organ.

The Sultan was exceedingly terrified by this event. His

secret police were set in action.   Hundreds of suspects were
arrested, tortured, and condemned without trial.   Some disappeared, some were exiled.   This only strengthened the
position of the Committee and added to the movement the
thrill of martyrdom.

·A plot organized by the Committee to depose the Sultan
and change the system of government was accidentally discovered.   New arrests followed.   Among those arrested
were many prominent men.   Kiazim Pasha, the commander
of the first army division, who was to be the chief ex-
ecutor of the plot was apprehended.   Many others were
exiled, but some managed to escape and join the revolutionary forces around Armed Riza Bey and Mourad Bey.
The attempt to establish new organizations in Constantinople failed, because most of the old members were
in prison, in exile, or else had met with violent deaths.
The medical school alone had maintained a strong organization, and kept publishing " underground " papers.
With their aid two new branches were organized at the
Military Academy.   In 1897, the students planned a demonstration before the palace.   It was discovered by the secret
police.   After horrible tortures, eighty-one of those arrested were condemned, thirteen to death.

While persecuting the suspects within the borders of the
country, Abdul Hamid spared no effort to check the movement abroad.   Not being able to bribe the leaders with
money or favors, he appealed to the foreign governments
to suppress the Young Turkish papers.   The French government consented in 1896 to suppress the *Meshverett* of
Ahmed Riza Bey and to expel the editor himself from
France.   This decision was later modified, as a result of agitation by the French press, only the " circulation of the
Young Turkish organ in France" being prohibited.   Ahmed
Riza Bey preferred to publish his paper in Switzerland,

but Abdul Hamid succeeded in bribing the printer and in buying the Turkish type which served for its printing [1] After publishing it for some time by lithography, the persevering journalist went to Belgium Being expelled from there in December 1897, he had to return to France.

Meanwhile, the Sultan had made a valuable acquisition to his *camarilla*, in the person of Izzet Pasha, a Syrian. This man whom Abdul Hamid called " the real friend he at last found " strengthened him in his pan-islamistic and fanatical tendencies, encouraging him to pursue his policy of the elimination and suppression of the undesirable in a larger measure, in spite of Europe and Young Turkey.

It was decided at the palace to try some new tactics against the Young Turks. Accordingly, they were promised all the reforms they wanted and a general amnesty, under the condition that they should cease their organization and propaganda work and give the throne opportunity to acquire some prestige for the coming reforms. Unless they accepted this, Abdul Hamid threatened to increase his persecutions and atrocities. Trusting in his promises and believing firmly that he was able to carry out his threats, the party was dissolved, all publications with the exception of *Meshverett*, suspended, and the leader Mourad Bey went to Constantinople as a hostage. He was personally honored and given a high position, a partial amnesty was proclaimed without being executed, but otherwise the Sultan showed no inclination to keep his word.

These happenings, especially the desertion of the most popular leader, had a depressing influence on the Young Turks. All hope was given up. The easy victory in the Greek-Turkish War of 1897 had also served to increase the

[1] Paul Fesh, *Les derniers jours d'Abdul Hamid* (Paris, 1907), pp. 336-337.

prestige of the Sultan as a military and religious lord, and made the period unfavorable for agitation.

The Young Turks in foreign countries were no longer centrally organized, but still individual efforts did not die out. The number of Young Turkish papers and the bulk of pamphlet literature were daily increasing. The *Mesh-verett* of March 15, 1898, speaks of seven new organs "established within the last two months." These papers were published mostly in Egypt, the Balkan States, France and Switzerland, and to a lesser extent in England, Germany, Austria and Belgium. Most of them were short-lived on account of financial difficulties, or on account of the fact that they were merely published to blackmail the Sultan. In 1898 and the following years, it was, in fact, the usual practice for ambitious functionaries without strong palace protection, to make a European trip as Young Turks, to publish, or to make an attempt to publish, mutinous literature, and then to sell their silence for a superior position in the government service.[1] There were also palace spies who lived in foreign countries disguised as Young Turks, in order to keep the Sultan informed about the doings of the revolutionary parties.

The Young Turkish papers were mostly published gratuitously. Everyone could get as many copies as he might ask for. They depended for their existence upon the personal means of the publisher, and on occasional contributions. Even those charging a subscription price were glad to send copies gratuitously on application. They had names such as "Constitution", "Liberty", "Safety", "Revival", "Justice", "Ideal", "Future", but names like "Thunderbolt", and "Revenge" could also be found. Most of them were of a political character, registering the events taking place

---

[1] *L'Etat Politique de la Turquie et le Parti Liberal,* pamphlet by Dr. J. Loutfi, Paris, 1901.

in Turkey behind the veil and discussing the methods of overthrowing the despotic government and of ruling the country after that overthrow. There were also satirical publications like *Davoul* (Kettle-Drum) and *Tokmak* (Mallet) Magazines of a serious character were rather small in number. The most prominent was the *Ijtihad* (Free Search) published by Dr. Abdullah Djevdet in Egypt. He also published a " Free Search Library " consisting of reprints of forbidden Turkish works and translations from French and English. Sociological works had a large share among the translated volumes of the library

At the beginning of 1900, the escape from Turkey of Mahmoud Pasha, a brother-in-law of the Sultan, with his two sons, and later of Ali Haidar Midhat Bey, son of Midhat Pasha, "martyr of liberty" as he is popularly called, made Young Turkey triumph anew at the expense of the Sultan

In 1902, forty-seven young Ottomans, belonging to the various elements of the population in Turkey, held a congress in Paris under the presidency of Prince Sabahiddin, eldest son of Mahmoud Pasha The Congress, which was primarily expected to find a basis for co-operation revealed the extent of agreement and disagreement existing between those who had revolted against the state of affairs in the country. In the face of the magnitude of the problems which invited their opposition, they almost appeared a homogeneous group They had in common the hatred against the Hamidian regime, the idea that the Sultan should be deposed, his dethroned brother Mourad proclaimed Sultan, and a constitutional regime established They had also in common the belief in the magical effect of the words " liberty, equality, fraternity." These magical words seemed to presage a complete metamorphosis and satisfied them in an easy way as to their future duties, since they could not analyze the real situation, and simply thought an overthrow of the existing system was all the work to be done.

Most of the recruits to the cause were students with ideals, or government employees who had experienced the evils of the system in their own cases. Theologians were also represented whose religious feelings were hurt by the backward state of the country, ascribed abroad to the influence of the Mohammedan religion itself.

The general type had deviations on both sides. On the one hand, there were those who found it fashionable and attractive to spend a merry life in Paris, and call themselves at the same time Young Turks and revolutionaries. On the other hand, there were earnest men who had a scientific training and a broad knowledge, who could understand and face the situation as it was.

All these men who seemed to have so many points of agreement in a general way, would hardly have been able to co-operate smoothly on the field of constructive action. They were mostly individualistic: even the most influential leaders had around them only a small circle of followers and adherents. Still, these men were able to maintain abroad a free Turkish political and intellectual life, and to keep afire, and strengthen through their literature the conscious efforts for betterment.

While this turbulent movement was developing abroad everything in Turkey seemed to lie dormant and stationary. In reality, this was so only on the surface. Two processes were taking place which were changing the outlook and the relation of things beneath the unchanging surface. The one was the growth of individuation, the other was the growth and specialization of the system designed to check this individuation because it might disturb the wide extent of power and full enjoyment of life of a single individual, Sultan Abdul Hamid.

Although Hashim Pasha, the Sultan's favorite minister for public instruction, had expressed the idea that his ministry could be run wonderfully, the budget balanced, the officials satisfied through large increases in their salaries, if only there were no schools to be taken care of, Abdul Hamid's greatest ambition was to be called by the press, as often as possible, " fosterer of public instruction " and " protector of progress ". He kept increasing the number of schools, but took pains that they should only check the " harmful tendencies noticeable in the new generation." In public schools of every description, not excepting the schools of agriculture and veterinary science, there were given courses in "morals" in which the students were taught that blind obedience to the Sultan and gratitude for his endless gifts were the supreme objects of life. To confirm the truth of these teachings, free board, and free clothing, and pocket money were given to the students of all higher institutions, agricultural, and industrial training schools, and to those students of secondary schools who could not support themselves. As an additional measure of precaution, the teaching of everything which might stimulate abstract thinking and produce idealists and dreamers was curtailed and attention concentrated on mathematics and the natural sciences.

The results were disastrous for Abdul Hamid. His free schools attracted a great many students from every class of people, but they produced only discontents and militants, who, profiting by their close association with other young men, could interchange revolutionary ideas. Very often there were attempts made to publish revolutionary papers in these closely guarded schools. After their graduation, the students carried the germ of revolt to every corner of the country, where they were sent as government officials.

'Besides this, the many thousands of exiles in the provinces were also engaged in active agitation. The foreign post-offices were the medium which broke the ban of isolation imposed by Sultan Abdul Hamid and brought in a life stream in the form of Young Turkish literature and French books. Without them the source of intellectual animation of Turkey would have been confined to works formerly written by Turkish authors and secretly circulated among those who were perfectly confident of each other's character. Many such works had never seen print; they existed only in manuscript or in memory. The present writer remembers having read the second volume of *Djezmi,* a historical novel which had never been printed, in a hand-written copy brought back by a cousin of his who had to do military service in the interior of Asia Minor.

Political exiles and other militant spirits who were obliged to use the old means of traveling by way of the road, stopping at inns overnight, found a peculiar outlet for the expression of their sentiments, in writing upon the whitewashed walls of their rooms such messages and ideas as they wished to communicate. Each traveler in turn read the utterances and added his own remarks to the thoughts of the previous writers, so that even in remote and isolated places, the flame of agitation was constantly fed.

In addition to the factors indicated so far, the economic changes, the increase in means of communication with Europe and the various parts of the empire, the growing importation of machinery and other manufactured articles, brought about a new distribution of energy, and a dislocation of current relations with need for readjustment. Instead of blind submission to authority, revolt and dissent began to be the quality admired and esteemed by many sections of the population. More pleasure began to be found in individual action and in change, than in following

the ways imposed by authority.   Questioning, doubt, self-
criticism made their way among such sections of the population where previously no worldly happening, no bitter experience could have disturbed the peace, harmony and submission to fate

'Hand in hand with this development grew the system
which aimed at suppressing it.   The group around the
Sultan became more and more intricate in its organization.
It was a hierarchy based upon favor and service   There
was a small number of men who enjoyed the personal
favor of the Sultan.   They all had their " men " whom they
appointed to important positions expecting from them part
of the booty and also expecting zealous effort for the maintenance of the system, manifested especially through denun-
ciation of those suspected of having " new " ideas.   The
" men " again had their dependents consisting mostly of
spies of varying degrees of importance.   As every party was
interested in acquainting the Sultan with more striking
material about the plots of the Young Turks, than his neigh-
bor produced, dramatic imagination was freely used, and
where evidence could not be found, it could be first arranged and then found.   Blackmail of every sort could of
course be very freely practiced under such conditions

The competitive zeal of the favorites and their " men ",
and the increasing signs of unrest resulted in making the
system more and more rigid and oppressive.   The books
published in one year were considered dangerous and were
forbidden during the next.   Every new day made people
look longingly back upon the previous day.   The experiences of former times when Midhat Pasha and Kemal Bey
were active and when there existed a free press, had gained
a mythical character in the public mind.   All who were
not actually in the system were against it.   When a few
people knowing each other perfectly well, could somewhere

come together where no spies could possibly be present, the stories of old times were repeated with patriotic passion. Conversations of this kind were often concluded with the words: "The Turks can never learn by experience. We can never be saved and reformed." In spite of these pessimistic words, everybody had the confident expectation in his heart that everything would be better as soon as the Sultan was overthrown. Such gatherings could not take place often, because social intercourse of every kind was considered suspicious and criminal. Even for wedding parties and gatherings of that sort it was safe to ask a secret policeman for his presence.

While the Young Turkish press issued in other countries gave expression to the individuating tendencies, the restraining efforts of the Hamidian system were reflected in the press published at home.

In 1891, when Young Turkish agitation against the Sultan began to gain a serious character, there were published in Constantinople, six dailies, (*Tarik, Terdjumani-i-Hakikat, Saadett, Servett, Sabah, Zuhour*), two political weeklies (*Mizan, Muruvvet*), a weekly military gazette, a weekly and a fortnightly navy gazette, weekly bulletins of justice, public works, and army medical service departments, a medical and a commercial review, an illustrated fortnightly, and a law review. The publications in non-Turkish languages included nine in Armenian, eight in Greek, two in French, two in French and English, three in Hebrew, one in German, one in Bulgarian, one in Persian and one in Arabic.[1]

After 1891, the Turkish press which was more and more restrained politically gave its entire attention to literary matters. The *Terjuman-i-Hakikat* and several other daily

[1] The official year book for 1891, chapter on the press.

papers became the scene of a remarkable literary movement, guided by men mostly belonging to the old generation. Some gifted writers of the young generation who had a thorough French training revolted against them and established a modern school, French in form, but Turkish in spirit. They founded an illustrated weekly named *Servet-i-Funoun* (Wealth of Knowledge). In spite of the imposed restrictions, this weekly created an intellectual revolution among the thinking classes, and influenced the present generation of Turkey more than any other single factor. Its poems, and short stories, and novels, analyzing critically the everyday aspect of the Turkish social life, were published in book form, in a series called the *New Literature Library*. In spite of repeated denunciations, the weekly was not suppressed, but managed to maintain its dominant position for several years, because its proprietor Ahmed Ihsan Bey was a classmate and friend of Arif Bey, a man high in Abdul Hamid's personal service. It found many imitators Even the provinces shared in the *New Literature* movement, among others, Brusa with the *Mouktebes,* Salonica with the *Mutalaha* and Smyrna with the *Haftalik Ismir.*

This movement was called a " decadence in literature and in social ideals," by the writers of the old school. The animosity between the old and the new was very bitter.

The opposition against the Young writers did not come only from a few colleagues who differed from them in ideas and principles The press had been invaded by a young man of great enterprising power who showed exceptional skill in becoming within a short time a palace favorite of influence. His name was Tahir Bey He was publishing four dailies, two in Turkish, one in French, one in Arabic, and five weeklies, and was threatening a complete monopoly of the Turkish press. He had introduced, for

the first time, yellow methods into the make-up and character of the Turkish press, where generally a conservative
and dignified tone was dominant. This man, who, in spite
of his tempting offers, could not add the adherents of the
new school to his staff, used his influence to restrain them,
and later to stop their activity altogether. The growth of
Young Turkish agitation abroad and the increase of autocratic tendencies by Abdul Hamid as a result of the easy
victory in the Greek War (1897) were factors which aided
Tahir Bey in his intrigues. His papers did not, however,
long retain their success; it was found out that he was
engaged in selling counterfeit orders and medals to ambitious foreigners, and his fall was as rapid as his rise. His
property was seized, and all his papers were suppressed.

This event did not give back to the remaining papers the
position they formerly enjoyed. Abdul Hamid's dread of
the press had so greatly increased that he did not authorize
the publication of a single new periodical in Constantinople,
during the decade preceding the Revolution of 1908. The
field had become crystallized in every respect. The only
changing element was the severity of censorship. Every
censor wanted to outdo the others in zeal. There was also
a great number of spies, who made the misprints in the
papers or peculiar interpretations of certain passages the
subject of their daily reports to the palace favorite, among
whose dependents they were.

The *Scrvet-i-Funoun,* the organ of the *New Literature
Movement,* was allowed to continue its existence under the
condition that it should, by no means, touch upon literature.
It could devote its space to medicine, agriculture, horticul-
ture, and to similar subjects. Poetry of every kind was
put under the ban, because " it might excite the feelings of
the people."

The single exception made, concerned poems in praise of
the Sultan and his work.

The only periodicals of literary character besides *Servet-ι-Funoun,* was a weekly for women and one for children. These papers had occupied an influential position at the time when the press was still allowed to publish original contributions of Turkish authors. At that time, there had been formed a staff of talented women writers, who kept their readers interested, even if they were not allowed to give expression to the ideas of feminism gaining ground among Turkish women. When signed articles were forbidden and even original contributions had to be published as translations from some foreign paper, the two weeklies would have discontinued their publications but for the subvention accorded them by the government

The rest of the periodical literature comprised only official publications of the state departments and the Chamber of Commerce.

Of dailies there were three the *Ikdam* (Perseverent Effort), the *Sabah* (Morning), and the *Terjuman-i-Hakikat* (Interpreter of Truth). The six dailies and two weeklies of 1891 had dwindled to this number, as the severity of censorship increased. All three received government subventions of about four hundred dollars monthly each Besides, the stamp tax had been abolished in 1900, when the relation of the press to the palace had become so close that there was no further need for financial restraint The price of all three papers was one cent per copy and eight dollars per year, postage prepaid. The *Ikdam* and the *Sabah* could support themselves even without the subvention, having a circulation of fifteen thousand and twelve thousand respectively. There was very little fluctuation in their circulation. In fact, the whole production in periodical literature under the Hamidian regime had been stationary in an absolute sense and widely retrogressive in a relative sense. While the number of the people with reading ability had tripled, and the price of the papers was reduced from four cents to one cent, nearly the same number of papers was circulated in 1873, as in 1901.

This can be proved, to some extent, by the number of press stamps consumed in the period between 1873 and 1901, when the papers had to affix a stamp of one-fifth of a cent on every copy.   The number was as follows: [1]

1873 (last five months)	19,304,360
1874	32,704,600
The yearly average for 1875-77	43,455,900
1878	55,702,440
The yearly average for 1879-81	47,772,340
The yearly average for 1882-84	50,906,540
The yearly average for 1885-87	54,435,000
The yearly average for 1888-90	59,167,700
The yearly average for 1891-93	58,435,000
The yearly average for 1894-96	62,435,500
The yearly average for 1897-1900	64,942,200

Unfortunately, the figures given here include the stamps used by papers in non-Turkish languages, as well as the large quantity consumed for printed matter having an advertising character.

The increase in the figures is undoubtedly due to the growth in the amount of printed matter for advertising purposes.   While, at the beginning, the stamp was almost entirely used by newspapers, the advertising circulars began later to use a larger and larger share.   This is shown by the fact that, in 1906, when all the papers were exempted from the stamp duty, the number of stamps sold for advertising literature still amounted to 55,600,440.

The necessity for issuing news rapidly and printing a

---

[1] The figures were kindly furnished by the Ottoman Public Debt Department.   They are not exact on the unit digit, because they were originally expressed in Turkish money value, and had to be reduced into numbers of stamps.

larger number of copies in a shorter time than usual during the Greek War of 1897, caused the technical equipment of the papers to be perfected. Their size grew, and their appearance improved The bulk of the advertisements also kept increasing, along with the economic activity of the country.

The situation was different, however, with regard to the contents of the papers. There the line of change was in the opposite direction On an average, one fourth of the space was given to official communications and news concerning the Sultan The rest of the internal news consisted of what was obtained by the reporters from the state departments. Crimes and accidents occupied very little space. The part of the paper really edited by the staff, consisted of translations or adaptations from foreign papers, and from the bulletins of telegraphic agencies. Every daily used to get a dozen or more French, Austrian, German and English reviews and papers. Everything found in them on foreign politics having nothing to do with Turkey and the European situation, and concerning mostly South America, the Far East and the Scandinavian countries, was translated, as well as cultural news of a harmless character and stories on odd happenings in different countries American millionaires formed a very popular subject to write about. The tendency to supply the elements of attraction which the papers generally lacked, by giving exaggerated tales on the doings of Americans was carried to such an excess that the word America became for the Turkish public synonymous with eccentricity and oddness Sometimes, imaginary happenings had to be presented as real ones, because fiction was, to a large extent, interdicted. At first, the interdiction concerned only the actions represented as happening in Turkey or among Turks. Later, every novel and story was prohibited which might

cause strong sensations.   Descriptions of travels were the
next thing to be singled out as permissible, love stories being put under a strict ban.

The policy of the palace was very rigid, but it was correspondingly short-sighted.   As the papers were not allowed to deal with matters of immediate interest to the
people, wild rumors of every kind could easily spread and
find credulous believers, in spite of the difficulties connected
with social intercourse   The papers which seemed to give all
their attention to inventing new titles and praising phrases
for the Sultan and which devoted their entire space for a
week or more after the anniversaries of the days of the
Sultan's birth and throne accession, to giving details of the
celebration and to describing how every single man of
prominence decorated his house, could not really enjoy much
prestige.   The readers were inclined to believe the opposite
of what the papers stated.   Whenever they reported with
insistence that public order in some part of the empire was
perfect, the readers knew by experience that some specially
grave trouble must have occurred there   Of course, there
was also a large class of readers who believed every single
word, and for whom a world outside of that marked out by
the papers did not exist.   Even these people, however,
would have taken their papers less seriously, had they
known how the passages relating to the Sultan were written.

The regular members of the staff of the paper would
have nothing to do with stories, in which the praise of the
Sultan was the main feature   Each paper had some old
experienced man to perform the work.   Only on rare
occasions, however, did even he have any amount of
original writing to do.   There were formulas in old
numbers fitting every possible case and event, in which
the Sultan might be involved.   These were simply
copied without any thought about their meaning and

sense. The copies were read twice by experienced copy readers who had the greatest responsibility regarding the destiny of the paper, and were the best paid men on the staff. The slightest misprint in a passage relating to the Sultan might have very grave consequences. A third reading of the copies was made by the censors who made an abundant and arbitrary use of their red ink. Although the journalists had a great deal of experience in judging between available and unavailable stories, one-fifth or more of the material presented was crossed out A certain number of copies, previously approved by the censors was always kept on hand for emergency cases.

♦The vocabulary used was very limited. As a large number of words could not be used, and as this number kept increasing, ability in paraphrasing became one of the necessary qualities of writing for the press. The journalists were always confronted with the temptation to use vague terms and to make people read between the lines. There was a conventional language used between the journalist and the experienced reader which made the latter learn more than the mere words could convey. For instance, when a foreign ruler became a victim of anarchists, the Turkish journalist wrote with insistence that he had died a natural death This insistent way of expression informed the reader that something was not quite in order.

It is remarkable that this corrupt press without any marked influence had a staff of very patriotic, honest and able men, although the proprietors in most instances were ready to accept every humiliation and sacrifice to gain favor and wealth The character of the profession had undoubtedly to do with this favorable selection, but the fact that newspaper work was very poorly paid also accounted for it. As people with elastic consciences, who had some writing ability, could easily ascend the scale, they could have no interest for this branch of work. The salary of a chief editor was about sixty dollars a month. An experienced editor received forty-five dollars and an ordinary translator twenty-five dollars. Reporters received from ten to thirty dollars a month. Most of them had outside occupations as tutors or government officials.

A peculiarity of the Turkish journalist was his number of titles and orders. The Sultan seemed to act according to the Turkish proverb, implying that it is wise to kiss the hand which one is not able to break. There were newspaper men who were given by the Sultan the title of " Excellency ", and some of the highest orders. There did not exist any journalist who had not his share in the distribution of titles and orders. Moreover, the Sultan abstained from giving the newspaper men personal causes for dissatisfaction. They were free to read foreign papers and to do many things, which the ordinary man could not do, without being molested by the secret police On the other hand, it was not wise for outsiders to have much to do with journalists. As they were in the " system " without actually belonging to it, and as they could read foreign papers, those seeking their company were likely to be denounced as committing a political offense.

While this atmosphere of imposed isolation which was calculated to undo and balance the social results of modern means of communication, was becoming more and more rigid and perfect, the disturbances underground were correspondingly increasing. This time Constantinople, where the palace was on its guard, was not made the centre of secret agitation. The Macedonian provinces which were under international control and where the government had sent a select and honest class of officials and army officers in order to demonstrate that it was capable of good government, were much more favorable fields of operation. The central organization of the *Committee of Union and Progress* was transferred to Macedonia from which place the revolutionary elements all over the country were guided and organized.

The concerted secret propaganda found so much favorable response from classes which had hitherto made submission their highest ideal, that the foreign papers often had occasion, in 1907, to report the startling signs of " unrest " in Turkey   The soldiers revolted in many places and asked the payment of their salaries in arrears, or demanded to be sent home after completing the time of military service required by law   People in various parts of Asia Minor rose to ask the dismissal of unpopular functionaries   The taxpayers who had suffered for generations every kind of oppression without any complaint refused to pay taxes, unless they were to be spent for their own benefit.   The inhabitants of Erzeroum declined to support financially the construction of a railway from Damascus to the holy places of Islam, on the ground that the railway was not of any use to themselves.   The fact that the Sultan was planning this railway as a pious act which would secure for him new prestige in the Mohammedan world, did not seem to impress the people of Erzeroum

The change of attitude was startling.   It meant that the efforts of the Sultan to counteract, through an artificial state of isolation, the effects of the redistribution of energy brought about by the growing contact with the industrial civilization of the West, and to maintain a medieval rule on partly modernized ground, had failed, even among the classes supposed to be fanatical and essentially submissive.

To the pressure of these circumstances, was added the fear that new territorial losses were imminent. unless rapid action was taken.

And the *Committee of Union and Progress* took rapid

action.   In July 1908, an open revolution was declared in
Macedonia.   After trying every means to crush it, and after
assuring himself that no escape was possible, the Sultan
yielded.   A constitution was proclaimed, and a new situation suddenly arose in Turkey.

CHAPTER V

THE PRESENT ERA

Part I   Developments since 1908 and their Interpretation

ON July 25, 1908, the dailies of Constantinople had an opportunity to make amends for their dubious activity of long decades.   On the previous day, they had published, without any heading, an official notice of three lines, to the effect that orders had been given to the provincial authorities to make arrangements for parliamentary elections.   As the great mass of the population was not informed about the real state of affairs, the satisfaction which the news created with the large majority did not find any immediate expression.   The journalists, to whom the reading of foreign papers was permitted, were better informed   They took the first steps towards stirring up the people   They were instrumental in causing some timid street demonstrations, and they forced the proprietors of the papers to decorate and illuminate the office buildings as a sign of rejoicing. In the evening, all Ottoman journalists gathered at a dinner to discuss the situation, and to lay the foundation of an " Ottoman Press Association ".   This step taken on the very first day of the new era characterizes the state of mind created by the sudden change, and the degree of its pressure.   Later, when the situation had become normal, repeated attempts were made to take further steps in organizing a press association, but no success could be attained beyond drafting a constitution.

The papers which appeared on July 25, were nothing but a fervent outcry of joy.   The censors who had usually had absolute sway in newspaper offices were even refused admittance that day.   Articles were published by popular writers who had not been allowed to use their pens for many years.

The effect was amazing.   The sleeping city became at once ablaze with excitement and enthusiasm.   The streets, where people did not usually even feel free to walk fast, lest they attract the attention of spies, were filled with noisy crowds, listening joyfully to revolutionary speeches, or making demonstrations before public buildings, newspaper offices, and foreign embassies.   Excepting towards the leading figures of the former government, a broad spirit of conciliation was displayed in every respect.   People belonging to different races and creeds who had always avoided friendly intercourse, took delight in fraternizing with one another.   Blame for the unconciliatory attitude they formerly showed was ascribed to the policy of the old government   " We loved each other, but the despotic government did not let us become aware of it ", were words to be heard in every part of the city, on that first day of enthusiasm.

Although the *Ikdam* had published about sixty and the *Sabah* forty thousand copies, the demand could not be met. In the afternoon, a copy of the *Ikdam* which was priced only one cent, could not be obtained from the newsboys for less than forty cents

In the following days, the enthusiasm kept increasing, gaining in extent and intensity, as the jubilant voices were echoed from every part of the empire, and from foreign countries.

A general craze for self-expression seemed to spring up Every one was inclined to celebrate the end " of the night-

mare of despotism and oppression " by speaking and writing in abundance.   The demonstrations and street speeches
were continuous   A bulky street literature in pamphlets,
pictures, and cartoons was created over night and found
wide circulation.   Within a few weeks, the number of Turkish dailies rose from three to as many as fifteen.   A new
class of comic publications was also established, ranging
between five and ten in number during the first months of
the new era   The number of publications in general was
highly shifting.   Every day some of the papers disappeared
to give place to new ones.   Only three of the new dailies
were edited by journalists of fame and proved capable of
supporting themselves, after the emotional outburst gradually died away   One of these three, the *Mizan* (Balance),
consisted of only four small pages, and contained nothing
beyond the personal opinions of Mourad Bey, the man who
had played a prominent part in the Young Turkish movement.   At times, this paper which made no attempt to give
news had a larger circulation than the well-founded newspapers.

•The dailies which did not succeed were generally founded
by men without any business experience, who had simply
followed the fashion of publishing a paper, or who sought
to acquire political prominence by publicity.   Some of the
more zealous men of enterprise thought that papers of every
shade and type, to be found in Western countries, had to
exist in the new and constitutional Turkey, to render her
modern equipment complete.   They accordingly established
papers which did not correspond with any existing need or
interest.   In this category belonged the communistic weekly
called *Ishtiraque* (Communism) which had this old Turkish
proverb as a motto.   "One eats, one looks,—there the
trouble broods "

The tendency for covering every possible line of publicity had, at the same time, some very happy results. A monthly review on economics and sociology came into existence and was more carefully edited and printed than many of the similar publications in other countries. There were other reviews of real scientific value like the *Istisharé* (Deliberation). Interest in women was demonstrated through the weekly *Demette* (Bunch of Flowers), and the *Mehassin* (Beauties), an extravagantly published illustrated monthly. The new Mohammedan attitude of mind towards religion found expression in the *Cirat-i-Mustekim* (Bridge of Righteousness). The numerous attempts to publish periodicals of a purely literary character failed. Popular illustrated magazines were more fortunate. Besides the *Servet-i-Funoun*, which was published under the old regime, the *Ressimli Kitab* (Illustrated Magazine), *Shehbal* (The longest pinion in a bird's wing), and *Kalem* (Pen) gained great success and popularity. The *Kalem* was a humorous publication of great artistic value and elegance of wit. This was in strong contrast to the rest of the similar publications which had to a great extent, a vulgar tone and which tried to·appeal to people who could not even follow and understand the daily papers.

Another group of publications consisted of the organs of different societies of a professional character, and of different sections of the student body. Almost simultaneously, there appeared organs for painters, architects, chemists, veterinary surgeons, physicians, lawyers, writers of different schools, actors, workingmen, government officials, former political exiles, alumni of the Civil Service School, and students. Nearly all of them were short-lived. The organizations they represented were not more fortunate in duration and stability. The motive behind them was not an innate, but only an imitative one. It was simply hoped that progress in a Western sense could be realized by adopt-

ing, without much critical examination, the forms and details of organizations which seemed to be the cause for the
superiority of the West

The procedure followed in every case—whether the society had to serve a public interest, a professional purpose,
or a business undertaking—was identical: the first thing
done was to find a brilliant name, then, a constitution was
drafted, which was in many cases, a translation of constitu-
tions of similar organizations in foreign countries. The
next step taken was a more or less pompous inauguration
ceremony The further life of the societies, depended
mostly on the existence or non-existence of a meeting-place.
Those fortunate enough to secure a meeting-place, had a
varying number of meetings, gradually declining in enthusiasm and interest Not even one, however, of the hasty organizations created during the first months of the new era,
could survive. Their great number is an index to the good
intentions and desire for activity produced through
the sudden political change, their failure, on the other
hand, demonstrates lack of deliberative like-mindedness and
possibility of co-operation even among people who were
drawn together by purposes and interests which they deemed
to be so strong as to warrant a formal organization
There are certain elements to be considered in order to
understand, why there was so much effort displayed in publications and organizations, and why so little success could
be achieved. In the first place, the ready example of the
West had so coercive an authority upon the minds of the
people that critical thinking and action according to the
existing circumstances were hampered Secondly, the pressure, both external and internal, demanding an immediate
regeneration could not, within the existing limits of equipment and organization, find other response than a change in
form and name. Thirdly, the Turkish elements of popula-

tion, as such, were the only ones in the country acutely interested in the welfare of the empire, although many individuals from other elements shared this interest. The Turks paid for their interest and for their position as a ruling race, very dearly and in manifold ways. For centuries in successive wars, they had lost their best and most courageous. In the struggle against authority, after the process of adaptation to Western ideas had begun, their most enlightened and enterprising men were eliminated. The great mass of the population, although oppressed by a palace *camarilla* consisting mostly of non-Turks, had the consciousness, if not the position, of a ruling race The majority of this population expected the government to do everything for them: to supply them with salaried positions, to educate them, to take care of their health, to furnish them with seeds and agricultural implements. Consequently the Turkish elements did not have opportunity for individual initiative, and could not gather experiences which would enable them to face a new situation. This deficiency was the price paid for the survival of the empire, which was constantly threatened from without and by a majority of the non-Turkish population, both Moslem and Christian, from within, and the very existence of which had become a miracle in the eyes of every foreign observer for more than two centuries.

A race which had given all its energy for survival and was, in consequence, obliged to be satisfied with living economically, and with sacrifice of individual enjoyments, under the strict sceptre of authority, could not afford to live, for any length of time, without following a dominating influence. There was no alternative in the new era. The nature of events assigned to the *Committee of Union and Progress* the rôle of control. The change brought about by the *Committee* was of great importance for all those who were not personally interested in the old system. With a single stroke it had done away with all those imposed restrictions against development and betterment which did not lie in the nature of the social situation. For the people in general, the success of the *Committee* meant much more than this They saw in it, not the opening of opportunities for change and betterment, but betterment itself. Therefore, there can be no wonder that the "sacred" *Committee* was deified by a large section of the people. They developed a Committee-mindedness and a Committee faith, which did not admit opposition and was in most instances incapable of critical consideration On account of this fact, and on account of the secret and attractive initiation ceremony, and the prestige and advantages connected with membership in the *Committee*, it could succeed highly as an organization. Branches were organized in every part of the country with the aid of government authority.

For some time, there was nothing to disturb the existing harmony. The people were busy with elections, which were made occasions of great festivity Pompous processions were formed to carry the ballot boxes through the city. The main features of such processions were a Mohammedan theologian with his white turban and a Christian priest in his black garb sitting together in a carriage. This was the accepted symbol of equality and "unity of elements". The general public which had demonstrated its interest for change, in changing the names of streets, schools, business concerns, shops, and in making a wide display of the national colors, cheerfully made this contribution to the new idea that all Ottomans, without distinction of race and creed, should form an undivided and harmonious whole. What they did, looked to them like real and lasting achievement. Gaining such great ends pleasurably and at a low cost, however, gave everybody so perfect a satisfaction that disappointment in a corresponding degree was bound to follow.

The declaration of Bulgarian independence and the annexation of Bosnia and Herzegovina by Austria were made new occasions for patriotic demonstration. A well-organized retaliatory action was taken in the form of a boycott of Austrian and Bulgarian goods. Even the red fez, the national headgear, which was largely manufactured in Austria was given up in this struggle, although, hitherto, the slightest modification in the shape and color of the headdress had not been tolerated. This action, although essentially impulsive in character, contained elements unprecedented in Turkish life. It meant resorting to self-aid by people who were accustomed to expect somebody else, their own government, or foreign powers, to act for them.

The territorial losses involved in the two incidents were only nominal. As the people were extremely sensitive regarding any kind of territorial loss, the dissatisfaction was still very great, when the two accomplished facts were sanctioned by the government through a wise compromise.

There were also other potential causes for dissatisfaction in this era. The regime of equality had put an end to certain privileges of nearly every element Especially the inhabitants of the capital, who had been systematically favored and spoiled by the Sultan, had to pay taxes and do military service. Furthermore, government employment was threatening to cease to be the general source of subsistence.

The reorganization of the state departments had caused to be driven out hundreds of functionaries who were incapable of making use, in the way of business enterprises, of the cash indemnity paid to them.

To the number of discontents produced by this state of affairs, were added ambitious men who did not want to play a less important rôle than those in power, nationalists belonging to the non-Turkish races, religious fanatics who were frightened by the sudden changes of the new era, and far-seeing patriots who could not approve of the secret activity of the Committee of " Union and Progress ", and its interference with the activity of responsible government officials.

The more or less forced downfall of the government of Kiamil Pasha, on February 14, 1909, aggravated the situation more and more, and made the approach of some kind of crisis imminent The Sultan, who had been left on his throne in order to avoid trouble, did not hesitate to take advantage of the situation through every possible kind of intrigue. He gave particular attention to securing influence with the press. His aim was directed to upholding the lack of restrictions to the activity of the press, and weakening every existing kind of control, and to creating anarchy.

It was easy to agitate along this line, because the press and a large section of the readers were blindly jealous of the liberties of speech and assemblage. In many instances, the courts were incapable of taking action against incriminated newspapers, because the public sympathy was strongly on the side of the press. It is remarkable that the press did not abuse its freedom as much as it might have done. Although people of a dubious character had found access to the press, personal attacks and blackmailing were relatively limited in amount. The prejudice against having matters of a strictly personal nature, especially family affairs given publicity had a strong restraining effect.

When the parliament proceeded to pass a press law which was a mere translation of the most liberal West-European laws, an outcry of protest arose throughout the country. The people were fond of resorting on every possible occasion to their new diversion of holding public meetings, listening to fervid speeches, and wiring to the competent authorities, and to the press their resolutions of protest. Demonstrations of this kind took place in great numbers to defend the " full liberty of the press."

As a result of the license arising from this state of affairs, the press reflected openly, or in a disguised way, the different contending currents, and interests.

Already, at the beginning of the new era, an artificial differentiation in political ideas and theories had been sought. The papers had felt obliged to adopt arbitrarily the lines of division existing in the European press. They had become radical, liberal, moderate, conservative, and so on. This part of the rules of the constitutional game, however, soon passed. The main line of division produced by the existing circumstances simply consisted of blind adherence and blind opposition to the *Committee of Union and Progress*, with a small, but increasing number of advocates of compromise. As the greater part of the population at the capital had reasons for being dissatisfied, all the Constantinople papers with the exception of two or three owned or directly controlled by the *Committee*, became opposition papers of varying degrees of bitterness. The press of European Turkey was on the side of the *Committee*. Especially the papers published in the regions where the Revolution had originally started, used merciless language against their opponents in Constantinople, and very strongly condemned " the intrigues woven in the miserable environment of old Byzantium." The press of Asia Minor was divided in its allegiance to the contending parties.

Both sides consisted of heterogeneous elements, having only the feeling of, and reason for, mutual opposition in common. Officially, the chief point in contest was the degree of local self-government to be given to the provinces.

Both parties used unfair methods to injure each other, methods which were often contrary to the customs of the country. Those who objected, were simply told that political parties in Europe. especially America, regularly used such methods, and that they were consequently part of the game. This argument had such an authoritative effect on people's minds that it could be used to sanction any kind of abuse A curious instance of this was the toleration displayed regarding the fanatical agitation of a daily called *Volcano* and secretly supported by the palace Although the dangers connected with such an agitation were clearly perceived, no action was taken against the *Volcano,* because " there existed clerical papers of the same nature in France and other European countries." On the same grounds the organization and public demonstrations of a reactionary *Mohammedan League* were tolerated

The atmosphere of Constantinople seemed to be full of explosives. In different parts of the provinces also, there had always been some kind or other of trouble and revolt Lack of control was noticeable everywhere. The extravagant waste of energy and the resulting social deficit prepared a situation where strong and restrictive action was bound to appear.

On April 5, 1909, Hassan Fehmi, the editor of the opposition daily *Serbesti,* was mysteriously shot on the street. The public was inclined to ascribe the act to the *Committee of Union and Progress* There could be no better basis for reactionary agitation against the government. The excitement soon reached a climax.

On April 14, Constantinople awoke to find the city under the control of military insurgents, who had previously driven away their officers and held a huge meeting to press their demands The whole thing was made to look like impulsive mob action. " We want the religious law to be applied." "We want an all-powerful Sultan: every herd must have a shepherd", were slogans passing from mouth to mouth. In reality, the movement was well organized, and kept under control all the time. There was almost no instance of pillage or excess, although thousands of armed soldiers went about in the streets for ten days. The leaders had been bribed by the palace, and they managed the mutiny with great skill. The only outrage committed was the destruction of the offices of the *Shoura-yi-Ummett* (Nation's Platform), a well-edited paper with a large staff of expert and prominent journalists, published directly by the *Committee,* and of the *Tanin* (Echo), another influential daily, which had voluntarily taken sides with the Committee

The population of the capital, and to a great extent even the press, were deceived, and took the event for a demonstration against the *Committee* rule, and for better and more liberal government. This view had at least to be expressed by the papers, which were every day visited and menaced by armed soldiers, who commented upon the contents of the day's issue, and gave instructions for the coming number.

The provinces thought differently about it. Many of them severed their allegiance to the Constantinople government, and within a week a Young Turkish army was within reach of Constantinople. The members of the Parliament retired to the army headquarters to sit as a " National Assembly ".

Meanwhile, the press of Constantinople had a week of vivid days and nights. Every move of the army relieved it more and more from the pressure of the soldiery to which it had been subjected Although the armed insurgents were still masters of the city, the papers soon felt free enough to discontinue their flattering tone. Later they began to remind the soldiers of the possibility of a Bulgarian invasion. in case they did not lay down their arms. Their tone took a warning and aggressive turn   The same procedure was followed regarding the Sultan himself   During the first days of the military Counter-Revolution, there were papers which used in regard to him almost the old-time phraseology and gave him a long list of deifying titles.   When the news reached the capital, that arrangements were made for action against the city, he began to be spoken of simply as " our Sultan ".   As soon as the army came near Constantinople, the " palace finger " and the " palace intrigues " were made subjects of daring remarks   At last, when the city was regularly besieged, the papers affirmed that " the great symbol of oppression and despotism was no more capable of further harmdoing."   The *Serbesti* (Liberty), the editor of which had been the journalist mysteriously killed only two weeks before, and which had openly accused the Young Turks of the act, now expressed the belief that its editor had undoubtedly been killed by the palace adherents in order to cast suspicion upon the Young Turkish *Committee* and mislead public opinion.   In spite of this changing attitude some of the opposition journalists found it safer to keep at large by flight before the revolutionary army entered the city.

On April 25, Constantinople was already in the hands of the Young Turks.   The Sultan was immediately deposed in accordance with the decision of the national assembly and of a *fatva* of the Sheik-ul-Islam, charging him with specific cases of cruelty and oppression

The first part of the experiment was now over.   The man whose existence influenced the situation unduly was eliminated from the field.   What was to come would be a product of existing circumstances, as modified by the authority of foreign example, national traditions, and the experiences of one year of free and constitutional government.

The new era marked the beginning of the end of the

Young Turkish idealism. Instead of sticking to the letter of
paper laws and the ideas of "liberty, equality and fraternity," constitutional rights were suspended through extraordinary measures, a state of siege was proclaimed, and
control by direct force, instead or by impression and
prestige, was sought. This has been almost uninterrupt-
edly the constitutional status of the county ever since, although its vigor went up and down rhythmically, to a great
extent through the interference of external dangers.

The new government held the press responsible for the
outbreak on April 13, 1909. Accordingly, the majority
of the opposition papers were suppressed, and most of the
members of their staff exiled. Those who had saved themselves by flight to Europe were condemned *in absentia.*
For some time opposition disappeared.

It did not take long to reappear however. Violent opposition was carried on through papers published in Paris
by political fugitives. The Turkish papers at home used
the margin of freedom left to them, to complain in a sharper
and sharper tone of the lack of abundant freedom They
were often suspended, but they soon found a way to get
around the difficulty. When they were suspended, they
simply reappeared the next day under a new name, re-
sembling as closely as possible the original name. If in addition, the responsible editor had to go to prison, the life
of the paper was not affected, because he was not a regular member of the staff. He was just paid to go to
prison when necessary, and it was not hard to find a new
" prison editor " The situation was closely similar to the
conditions in the French press, under the second Empire

In spite of the protests of some of the papers, the military regime proved efficient, and productive of constructive
work, as long as it was able to maintain itself. The parliament worked with great zeal and passed, within a short

time, a long list of laws. Every branch of government was in full activity. Special attention was given to public instruction, and a large number of students were sent abroad

Unfortunately there were elements in the situation which began to temper the maintenance of a perfect and harmonious control, as soon as the overwhelming impression produced by the happenings of April 1909, lost its freshness and its vigor. The main element of weakness consisted in the fact that the real authority rested with the irresponsible secret *Committee* and not with responsible agencies As a consequence of the interference and secret and personal acts of the *Committee*, the military regime soon began to lose the prestige and support it enjoyed.

On the other hand, the Counter-revolution of April 13, 1909, had confirmed the idea of the *Committee* leaders that they, as the originators of the Revolution of 1908, had to watch over the destinies of the Empire and save it from all destructive tendencies To be able to play such a rôle, power and influence were considered necessary. The methods followed by the dethroned Sultan to gain power were still fresh in the minds as tempting examples. Unconsciously the *Committee* leaders began to follow them more and more closely, but with the great difference that the Young Turks were sincere, and to a great extent, disinterested and self-sacrificing patriots, who were, even in their gravest blunders and mistakes, influenced more by their over-zealous patriotism than by a conscious lust of power. Full advantage was taken of the impressive effect of secrecy and mystery Religion was used as a basis of agitation to secure popularity Worst of all a blind and aggressive Turkish imperialism became the dominating motive of the *Committee's* policy. Phrases like " Ottomanism ", and the " unity of all elements of population in Turkey without dis-

tinction of creed and religion " were still cited; but the
meaning given to them was no longer the meeting of the
different elements on a common and neutral ground through
mutual sacrifice as citizens of the Ottoman Empire pos-
sessing equal rights. They were simply assumed to
mean assimilating the non-Turkish elements of the
population through coercive methods, if necessary. The
conclusions prompting the recourse to coercive methods were generally reached through abstract reasoning
as to the rights and duties of the citizens of a state
in general, disregarding the existing circumstances and
handicaps. Such a policy could not work. It served only
to strengthen the artificial barriers between the Turks and
the non-Turks who had become closely similar in their folk-
ways and habits as a result of common environment and
centuries of intercourse. Through a tactful and concilia-
tory policy, a working degree of goodwill and co-operation
might easily have been established between them, and a
great amount of conflict and waste avoided. Instead, the
harsh policy followed, produced repeated revolts in Albania
and other parts of the Empire, the pitiless oppression of
which brought about great losses in life and property. A
large majority of non-Turkish elements became more aggressively hostile than they had been previously, to the very
existence of the empire.

   This tactless attitude was also extended to foreign relations. Although the Island of Crete had long been lost to
Turkey, the right of hoisting a Turkish flag at Suda Bay
being the only remaining trace of Turkish dominion, and
although there was no hope of winning back more positive
rights of sovereignty, a tremendous agitation was made for
the sake of the island   Emotional appeals were made and
meetings called everywhere to affirm that " thirty million
Ottomans would rather die together than give up an inch

of that sacred and dear soil " The papers were full of patriotic telegrams from every part of the Empire competing
with each other in the vigor of their language — Crete was
made an idol which ate up all the energies and all the enthusiasm the people could devote to public matters.   As the
great majority of the Turkish population was extremely sensitive regarding territorial gains and losses, the words spent.
and reflected through public channels, in behalf of the
" sacred " island, gave everybody a deep sense of satisfaction and achievement at an extremely low cost.   Besides,
the emotions systematically worked up and intensified
through every possible social agency, produced a subjective
atmosphere of self-confidence and feeling of invincibility
and power. which made public opinion assume an attitude
of challenge to neighboring states, and even to great powers

·The imperialistic and self-deceiving tendencies were reflected in a very aggressive way in a group of papers which
sprang up in the parts of European Turkey where the
Revolution of 1908 first broke out.   They were published
by retired army officers and ex-revolutionaries. and bore
names like " Weapon ", " Sword ", " Bayonet ", " Bullet ",
and " Thunderbolt ".   These few words, published by the
Silah (Weapon) [1] as an answer to an article of a Bulgarian
semi-official paper, advocating friendly relations with
Turkey are characteristic of the attitude of this type of publications:

We can become friends with whomever we desire to   Only
we cannot make friends with Bulgarians, as long as they continue to be mere brigands.   Lions can associate themselves only
with tigers.   A nation composed of lions, a great power, cannot become the friend of a cat youngster like Bulgaria.

Although chauvinistic conceit had been manifested on

_____
[1] Salonica, September 12, 1911.

several occasions by the Turkish press in general, its development to such a degree and in such a tone was unprecedented, and constituted an extreme deviation from the habitual tolerant attitude of the Turkish mind. Such conditions were alarming signs of social peril, if not of social degeneration. In a country without proper schemes of organization and at the margin of social deficit, the combination of a wasteful imperialistic policy with opportunities and pressure for individualistic self-betterment and a relatively large measure of free discussion was bound to have fatal effects. It is futile to hold the leaders of the *Committee* or anybody else responsible for the situation. In a state of instability, and a widespread struggle for survival, there was small place for rational and deliberative men. The circumstances were such as to put forward daring men of action of ideo-emotional and dogmatic-emotional types as the real leaders. Where no binding traditions, tested experience and inter-acting organizations, existed, and the right way had to be found through experiment, leaders of that type, even if they were self-denying and sincere men, were likely to commit arbitrary and irresponsible acts and grave mistakes.

As a consequence, the moderate and deliberative elements began to desert the *Committee's* ranks and join hands with the elements who had varying reasons for discontent. In the parliament which originally consisted of the *Committee's* candidates, the opposition factions secured a working majority. They organized themselves as the party of *Liberal Union*. It soon became apparent, however, that the new party was not different from its opponents in its composition and tactics. In order to secure a great numerical success, even people who had never gained access to the ranks of the *Committee* were enlisted as adherents. Irresponsible elements became more and more

prominent, and a worse sort of political fanaticism and in-
tolerance was developed than was formerly attributed to
the *Committee*.

The animosity between the two parties was extremely
strong. Each side considered the opponents traitors who
had only their personal interests at heart, and who were
capable of destroying the country to further their personal
ambitions. On July 29, 1909, Samim Bey, of the *Sedayi-
Millet* (Voice of the People), a paper published by Cos-
midis Effendi, one of the Greek deputies for Constantinople,
and on July 11, 1911, Zekki Bey, who was a contributor to
Alemdar (Standard Bearer), were mysteriously shot in the
streets, after being warned and threatened beforehand by
anonymous letters. The excesses in the provinces were
general and more numerous. Those suspected of holding
views in opposition to the *Committee*, or of simply reading
papers of the opposition, such as *Yeni-Gazetta* and *Ikdam*,
especially *Alemdar* and *Tanzimat* were subjected in many
instances, to violence and maltreatment. Although the government showed a mark of favor to the press in 1909 by
exempting it from the postal monopoly and thus enabling
the papers to make their shipments to the provinces at regular freight rates, only government papers such as *Tanin*
and the independent *Sabah* could take full advantage of this
favor, as the opposition papers were barred out by the
Committee branch organizations, and the dependent local
governments, from most parts of the country. It is
of interest to note that those who were so aggressively
intolerant of criticism and opposition, maintained on every
occasion that criticism and opposition were the essential
elements of constitutional government; they often cited the
words of the popular writer Kemal Bey to the effect that
" the sparkle of truth is produced only by a conflict of
ideas." What they could not tolerate, they asserted, was
the particular kind of criticism existing in Turkey.

The rational and moderate elements, foreseeing that violence and oppression could only cause explosive feelings to accummulate, which would burst out some day at the cost of the country, protested against the existing state of affairs and made repeated attempts to bring about a compromise.

The old publicist Ebouz-Zia Bey, officially a member of the government party in the parliament, made the following utterance in the weekly he published:

There is an old proverb in Turkish, "strong vinegar eats up its own dish". This proverb will verify itself in regard to the government and her violent press policy. It must be understood that the press is a very dangerous thing to play with. If the stream of public opinion is brought to overflow, every effort to narrow its channel increases its force, and makes it carry away those who are responsible. We would not pity them for getting their well deserved punishment, unless we had to think of our unfortunate country which needs peace and rest.

Among these attempts to bring about compromise and moderation, the most conspicuous was the association established by a number of university graduates for the purpose of producing rational currents of opinion by scientific methods, and thus removing the unsound and harmful elements from the situation. Considering it necessary to give the people, first of all, a practical lesson in private initiative, they founded a boarding-house connected with a literary club, a restaurant, a grocery store, a book shop, and a publishing business. Beginning December 9, 1911, the weekly *Vasifé* (Duty) was published as their organ. The young men were able to stimulate a great deal of attention and sympathy through their activity and sound views. Still, the undertaking was short-lived, on account of financial difficulties and friction with the government.

There was more reality underlying the efforts of the papers published in the agricultural regions of Asia Minor, like the *Keuily* (Peasant) of Smyrna and the *Babalik* (Adopted Father) of Konia, to do away with the destructive contest ravaging the meagre supply of working energy the country possessed   They constantly used the defects in the agrarian situation as an argument in urging " that the political leaders had no right to indulge in pleasurable and exciting political games, while the peasant who for centuries had given his blood and labor for the survival of the Empire was suffering heavily under his many burdens "

Such appeals to reason were gladly quoted by the papers of both parties to injure the other side, but the conflict continued unabated.

The outbreak of the war with Italy, and the loss of prestige connected with it, changed the balance of power against the *Committee of Union and Progress*   The parliament was dissolved with the hope that order and control might be restored by eliminating the opposition factions from the new parliament through coercive electioneering.

This hope was not realized   The outcome, instead, was a series of revolts in various parts of the Empire, especially in Albania.   A large number of army officers, organized as a " group of deliverers ", thought it necessary to interfere with those in power, and the *Committee* government was forced to retire.

The new government was composed of men of integrity, enjoying general confidence and prestige.   The independent and opposition papers (*Sabah, Ikdam. Yeni-Gazetta, Tanzimat*) proclaimed in a triumphant and jubilant tone that " the constitutional regime and full liberty of thought were restored "   The parliament consisting of the appointees of the *Committee* was immediately dissolved Stimulated by the critical situation the government began a zealous campaign to put the national house in order.

It was too late. The disturbed situation and the loss of prestige and power of impression connected with it, which had made the Italian invasion of Tripoli possible, had already prepared the way for another foreign invasion.

In October 1912, the Balkan War broke out. Turkey was caught unprepared because the new government had to begin its work by reorganizing many things in the army and other branches of administration. Besides, the party which had within its ranks the most ardent nationalists and militarists and which had always displayed resourcefulness and power for agitation and organization in times of high pressure was now an opposition party. At the outbreak of the war the opponents fraternized, of course, in a very demonstrative way, and assured each other that no feud or animosity should exist between them, as long as the war lasted. Still, no real solidarity could be established and a general national enthusiasm could not be aroused.

When at last, the government was obliged to sign a treaty establishing a humiliating peace, the *Young Turkish Committee* stepped in, easily mastered the situation, and regained a considerable amount of prestige in the second Balkan War, which enabled Turkey to reoccupy the City of Adrianople.

From the standpoint of Turkey's future as a nation the Balkan War could not have closed in a way more likely in the end to retrieve prestige. Far-reaching benefits were secured in the way of self-realization and self-consciousness through defeats and humiliations. The loss to self-confidence and the hope of national survival, a natural outcome of crushing defeat, was greatly alleviated, through the prestige resulting from the reoccupation of Adrianople

This was not quite apparent at first sight. The war had given occasion to outbursts of patriotism, even of fanaticism. The Turcophobe policy followed by the foreign powers, and prejudices shown against Turkey in all Christian countries had caused such strong reactions, that one might be justified in thinking that this war had thrown Turkey back many decades in the way of rational awakening and progress. It is true that the attitude of Europe had aroused bitter feelings even among the people who could not ordinarily be classed as chauvinists. Jenab Shehabiddine Bey, a popular poet, on July 7, 1913, published in the short-lived daily *Azm* (Determination), a long article under the heading of " a letter to my son ", which ended as follows:

We have been defeated, we have been shown hostility by the outside world, because we have become too deliberative, too cultured, too refined in our conceptions of right and wrong, of humanity and civilization. The example of the Bulgarian army has taught us that every soldier facing the enemy must return to the days of barbarism, must have thirst of blood, must be merciless in slaughtering children and women, old and weak, must disregard others' property, life and honor. Let us spread blood, suffering, wrong and mourning. We may only thus become the favorites of the civilized world like King Ferdinand's army.

In spite of the fact that feelings of this sort often found expression, the real effect of the Balkan War was in the opposite direction. It built up a new situation in which change and progress could find a course of development, entirely unprecedented in the history of modern Turkey. The defeat in the war, had proved the inefficiency of the modern building erected on the old foundation, through an imitative process and the employment of new words, forms and manners. It had subjected everybody to a long and subversive mental crisis, demonstrating plainly that something was wrong, that something had to be changed, and changed quickly and thoroughly. Mahmoud Sadık Bey, one of the ablest Turkish journalists, expresses the idea very frankly in the *Ikdam* (April 2, 1913):

The defeat has demonstrated that the ways we have followed up to now do not lead anywhere. It has shown us that we have to get rid of our errors and mistakes, of our conceit, of our haughtiness, confess our ignorance and incompetence, and seek sincerely and energetically for the right way, for the way of deliverance. We must not be satisfied with half-measures, with half-knowledge, with half-education. These have been the greatest cause of our disasters. They have obscured our view as to the real situation and made us self-satisfied, conceited and stationary.

The *Sabah* makes the following utterance on the subject:

Whatever the material losses of the war may have been, there can be no doubt about the moral benefits it brought about for us. It has created a new sort of self-realization, it has given a new direction to our national life, it has done away with the last barriers between us and modern progress. In short, our defeat means the final victory of modernism in Turkey.

In fact, the new attitude of mind created by the recent happenings and by the systematic activity of the press have become apparent in every branch of life. To cite an illustration, nobody, during the war, thought of objecting to the public activity of women, their caring for the wounded, or their meetings and public demonstrations. The activity of papers such as the *Women's World*, entirely edited by women, in critically discussing the shortcomings of the Turkish social life, is to-day, at least tolerated by everybody, even if disapproved of by many. Within the few months following the end of the war, several new institutions of learning for women were founded. At the present time the papers complain freely of the small number of Turkish girls studying at European Universities, and urge the government to admit women to professional schools. As a first result of this agitation, some special courses for women have been arranged at Constantinople University. What is even more interesting, Belkis Shevket Hanoum, one of the editors of the *Women's World* recently took a ride in a military aeroplane, throwing down upon the assembled throng, feministic literature. This woman was afterwards spoken of by the press as a popular heroine, and the government has decided that her picture shall be kept at the military museum. Such changes were not even dreamed of a year ago.

Another interesting change which may serve here as a further illustration is seen in the critical attitude taken towards religion. Before the war, religion was excluded from any critical discussion. Such ignorant theologians as were averse to progress could at most be referred to as " some people of ignorance who cannot understand the needs of the time " Even the most enlightened and rational papers felt obliged to publish on the birthday of Mohammed and on similar religious occasions, notes of praise and devotion at the top of their first page, in a formal and complex phraseology, unintelligible to most of the readers. Very few read them, and only a limited number were conscious of their meaning Omission to do this, caused the *Yeni-Gazetta*, one of the dailies published until recently, to be boycotted in 1909 by a large section of its readers, who mostly asserted that they did not mind the blunder themselves, but merely feared, in the name of public order, the shocking effect it might have on the " general public."

After the war, on the other hand, the *Idjtihad* (Free Search) felt at liberty to publish a series of articles entitled " Was Mohammed an Epileptic ?", and another series under the title of "War on Theologians". Abdullah Jevdet

Bey, the proprietor of this same weekly had been severely attacked and persecuted two years previously for having translated a French scientific treatise on Mohammedanism. At that time, no Turkish paper had dared to utter a word of defense in his behalf!

The critical attitude towards religion is no longer destructive. Formerly, nearly every man of any education took pride in asserting that he felt himself above the need of religion and wanted to have nothing to do with it. Now the importance of Mohammedanism as a secondary source of social energy is fully realized. It is generally understood that progress is only possible by adapting both people and institutions to the new situation, instead of abandoning the institutions and imitating the West in a loose and rather individualistic way.

Furthermore, an additional source of social energy is being created by building up a purely Turkish nationalism. A society called *The Turk Yourdou* (Turkish Home) is the most successful and lasting institution in Turkey, with the exception of political organizations. It is publishing several periodicals with the idea of simplifying the language, creating a responsive Turkish social mind, reviving popular poetry, myths and folklore, and establishing in general, a new cord between the educated and uneducated classes, who had become strangers to each other, through the lack of intercourse, under the former rule of the dethroned Sultan. A weekly called *Halka Dogrou* (Towards the Masses) is published for this special purpose.

The tremendous changes thus manifested indicate plainly that the unfavorable and deficient balance between the waste and repair of national energy must have been replaced by a sounder state of affairs. In fact, such a process actually took place through the loss of Macedonia, Albania, and other European possessions of Turkey These regions, peopled to a great extent by heterogeneous and troublesome elements, kindred racially and religiously of the neighboring Balkan states, threatened from every side by external dangers, and very hard and costly to be kept and defended, absorbed the best part of Turkish energy, and did not give Turkey opportunity to direct her efforts very much beyond a struggle for survival. A militaristic policy, a reign of terror under constitutional forms were the results.

Had the Turks had less energy and vitality, had they been less fortunate and successful in holding, in spite of their small number, a vast imperial system, threatened externally, a real storehouse of heterogeneous elements internally, they would not have been obliged to give up every possibility of individuation, to stick to a military and despotic government to prolong their existence, and to give Mohammedanism a settled and stationary form, in order to make it a prop of their inertia.

As matters stood, the release of Turkey from stationary conditions and her development on modern lines could only be possible by a decrease of the imperial burden. As a matter of fact, Turkey, thought to be about to expire at the end of the eighteenth century, came out stronger from every loss of territory. Especially since the recent instance of loss, when a good piece of troublesome ballast was passed on for other national craft to carry, social development has taken a strongly ascending course.

Never before in Turkish history were the evils and shortcomings of the nation so frankly exposed, constructive criticism so welcome, men and women alike provided with such vast opportunities for individuation, as after the Balkan War as a result of the amputation of the sick and energy-absorbing parts of the territory.

This is not yet apparent at every point, however, because many signs of the recent crisis are still prevalent, and some personal and traditional elements persist

*Part II.   Number, Contents and Character of Turkish
Papers in the Present Era—Their Relations to the Readers in the Light of a Questionnaire*

The Turkish press of to-day is marked by the relatively
small number of dailies and the large number of reviews devoted to special purposes and lines of interest.   Their policy
and contents indicate that instability, unrest, agitation, and
militancy, caused by social deficit, are being followed by
earnest and constructive effort, a sign of the coming of a
more fortunate balance between waste and repair.

For the purpose of comparison and illustration, a classified list of all Turkish periodicals published in Constantinople at the end of 1911 and of 1913 is given below.   It
was kindly supplied by the press bureau of Turkey.[1]

Dailies

1911	1913
Tanin (Echo)	*Tanin* (6, rarely 8 pages)
Sabah (Morning)	*Sabah* (4 pages of seven col-
Ikdam (Perservering Effort)	umns each)
Terdjuman-i-Hakikat	*Ikdam* (6, rarely 8 pages)
(Interpreter of Truth)	*Terdjuman-i-Hakikat*
Yeni-Gazetta (New Journal)	(4 pages)
Bedahett (Evidence)	*Tasfir-i-Efkiar* (Tablet of
Teshkilat (Organization)	Thoughts, 6 pages)
Tchigir (New Way)	*Ifham* (Explanation, 4 pages)
Kader (Destiny)	

Humorous

Kara-Gheuz (Punch)	*Kara-Gheuz* (Semi-weekly)
Ghévézé (Babbler)	*Souffleur* (Prompter)
Keuily (Villager)	*Yegh-Bun* (Stupid)
Tokmak (Mallet)	
Perdé (Curtain)	
Yenitchéri (Janissary)	
Munassibdir Effindim (It is	
alright, Sir!)	

[1] According to official estimates the number of those who declared
their intention to the press bureau, of publishing periodicals, from
July, 1908, to December, 1911, amounted to more than two thousand.
Many of these publications never appeared.

Illustrated Magazines

1911	1913
(Weekly) *Servet-i-Funoun* (Wealth of Knowledge)	*Servet-i-Funoun* [1]
(Fortnightly) *Shehbal*	*Shehbal* [2]
(Monthly) *Ressimili Kıtab* (Illustrated Book)	*Ressımili Kıtab* [3]
	(Weekly) *Rebab* (Tambourine)
	(Weekly) *Edman* (Sport)

Popular and Nationalistic

Turk Yourdou (Turkish Home)	*Turk Yourdou*
Mejmou'a-i-Ebouzzia Ebouzzıa's Review)	*Buyough Doigou* (Lofty Feeling)
Vazifé (Duty)	*Halka Dogrou* (Towards the Masses)
Ahval-A'zira (Present Situation)	*Turk Doigoussou* (Turkish Feelings)
Hayat (Life)	*Djérıdéı-Havadıs* (Register of News)
Yurek (Heart)	*Yénı-Touran* (New Touran[4])

School and Children

Tchotchouk Duniassi (Children's World)

Ghenjlik Alemi (Youth's Universe)

Mekteb Muzessi (School Museum)

Mektebli (Pupil)

Talébé Deftéri (Pupıl's Notebook)

Tchojouk Doigoussou (Children's Feelings)

Tchojouk Yourdou (Children's Home)

Tchojouk Derneghi (Children's Assembly)

[1] Of more than 32 pages, of the type of Parıs *Illustration.*

[2] Careful and discrimınatıng publication of the type of the London *Graphıc*

[3] Similar to ordınary Amerıcan Monthly Magazınes

[4] According to Persian legends the orıginal home of the Turks.

1911

1913
Tchojouk Hayati
  (Children's Life)
Mekteb Alemi
  (School World)
Tchalishalime! (Let Us
  Work)

Women

Kadinlar Duniassi [1]
  (Woman's World)
Kadinlik Hayati
  Life of Womenhood)

Religious

Cirat-i-Mustekim
  (Bridge of Righteousness)
Beyan-ul-Hak
  (Statement of Truth)
Tesav-vouf
  (Spiritual Philosophy)
Mihver-ul-Ouloum
  (Centre of Knowledge)

Sebil-ur-Reshad
  (The Right Path)
Djeridéï-Soufié
  (Journal of Sufism)
Islam Dunyassi
  (Islamic World)
Elmedariss
  (Religious Seminars)
Medréssé I'tikadlari
  (Seminar Dogmas)
Ghelimé-i-Taïbé
  (Good Word)

Professional

Mehamatt [2] (Defense)
Tijarett Odassi Gazzetassi [3]
Ghenj Tabib
  (Young Physician)
Ghenj Muhendiss
  (Young Engineer)
*Ressamlar Jem'ietti Gazzet-
  tassi* [4]

Mehamatt
Tijarett Odassi Gazzetassi
Ghemidji (Sailor)
Ghenj Muhendiss

---

[1] An illustrated weekly of the size of Harper's Weekly, entirely edited by women.

[2] Organ of the Constantinople Bar.

[3] Journal of the Chamber of Commerce.

[4] Gazette of the Painters' Society.

Agricultural

1911   **1913**

Zıra'att Gazetassi
    (Agricultural Gazette)
Eghinji (Husbandman)
Toprak (Earth)
Felahat (Cultivation)
Tavoukjulik
    (Poultry Journal)

Military and Naval

Mudaféa-i-Mılı'é   *Mudaféa-i-Mılı'é*
    (National Defense)   (With a French Edition)
Gheunullu (Volunteer)   *Deniz* (Sea)
Gavassé (Submarine)   *Gavassé*
Donanma (Navy)   *Donanma*
                                  Altoun Ordou
                                      (Golden Army)

Scientific

Riyaziyatt (Mathematics)   *Idjtihad* (Free Search)
Tebabett-i-Hazira   *Yeni-Fıkir* (New Thought)
    (Modern Medicine)   *Tarıh Enjuméni*
Tarih Enjuméni   *Mejmouhassi*
    Mejmouhassi[1]   *Fen vé San'att*
                                      (Science and Art)
                                  Felséfé Mejmouhassi
                                      (Journal of Philosophy)
                                  Yéni-Bılghı
                                      (Modern Knowledge)
                                  Seririat Mejmouhassi
                                      (Medical Review)

Besides the self-supporting publications enumerated above, there are eight weeklies published by the departments of war, navy, justice, agriculture, public works, and the daily *Takvım-i-vekayih* (Calendar of Events) issued by the ministry of the interior.

---

[1] Journals of the Historical Society

The publications in non-Turkish languages are as follows:

	1911		1913	
	Dailies	*Periodicals*	*Dailies*	*Periodicals*
French	6	8	5	5
Greek	7	6	6	12
Armenian	5	11	6	17
Arabic	1	1		3
English				
(Partly in French)	1		1	
German				
(Partly in French)	1		1	
Bulgarian		1		
Hebrew		1		4
Persian				1

While two or three years ago very few of the provincial towns had any publications besides the official weeklies, there are now self-supporting papers even in smaller towns outside of the seats of the provinces. There is a general tendency in most of the provinces to make themselves independent of Constantinople, and to create a local atmosphere of their own. From the viewpoint of the Turkish press, the most important centers are Smyrna, Brusa, Konia and Trebizonde. Smyrna has besides the Official Gazette, and thirteen Greek, five French, five Hebrew, and two Armenian papers, the following publications in Turkish: *Hidmett* (Service), *Ahengh* (Harmony), *Anadolou* (Anatolia), *Keulu* (Peasant), *Teshhir* (Exposing), *Al Sanjah* (Red Flag), *Tatbikat* (Practice), *Sanihat* (Inspirations), *Mulhakat* (Country News), and *Manissa* (The Town of Magnesia).

In Konia there are published: *Hakkem* (Arbitrator). *Meshrek-i-Irfan* (Dawn of Enlightenment), *Babalik* (Adopted Father), *Meram* (Determination), *Ouf-ki-Ati* (Horizon of Future), and *Yeni-Tchiftchi* (Modern Farmer).

In Brusa, appear *Ertougroul* (name of the father of the first Turkish Sultan), *Broussa, Mudafa'a* (Defense), *Mujahid* (Seeker), *Barika-i-Irshad* (Lightening of Enlightenment) ; besides, the Town of Eski-Shehir in the same province has a Turkish paper, *Hakikat* (Truth), and Aıvalik, a Greek paper.

The number of papers in other provinces is as follows:

	Turkish	*Greek*	*Armenian*	*Arabic*	*Other Language*
Adana	4	—	—	—	—
Adrianople	5	1	—	—	—
Aleppo	7	—	—	5	—
Angora	4	—	1	—	—
Bagdad	5	—	—	19	—
Basra	2	—	—	6	—
Beyrouth	1	—	—	41	—
Dardanelles	2	1	—	—	—
Dıar-Bekir	5	—	2	—	—
Erzeroum	3	—	2	—	—
Harpout	3	—	1	1	—
Hıjaz (Mekka) .	1 [1]	—	—	—	—
Jerusalem	1	—	—	15	3 [2]
Kastamani	3	—	—	—	—
Mousoul	3	—	—	2	—
Sivas	3	—	7	—	—
Syria	1	—	—	26	—
Trebizonde	11	3	1	—	1 [3]
Van	1	—	3	—	—
Yemen	1 [4]				

In the provinces lost to Turkey, the following number of papers were published before the foreign invasion:

[1] Turkish and Arabic.

[2] 2 French, 1 Hebrew.

[3] French.

[4] Turkish and Arabic.

	Turkish	Greek	Bulgarian	French	Other Languages
Archipal	1	4	—	—	—
Kossova	4	—	—	—	—
Monsatir	2	—	—	—	—
Salonica	11	1	1	2	5 (Hebrew)
Scutari	4	—	—	—	1 (Albanian)
Tripoli	2	—	—	—	2 (Arabic)
Yanina	3	1	—	—	3 (Albanian)

The entire number of periodical publications within the Ottoman dominions at the end of the year 1913, was three hundred and eighty-nine. Periodicals published by foreign societies, chambers of commerce, and colleges were not included in the number. Of these three hundred and eighty-nine, one hundred and sixty-one were in Turkish, (seventy-one of them published in Constantinople including eight official weeklies and a daily), one hundred and eighteen in Arabic, forty-two in Armenian, thirty-eight in Greek, eighteen in French, ten in Hebrew, one each in English, German, and Persian.

As conditions in Turkey are not yet settled, any extraordinary event may cause an abnormally large increase in the number of papers and again there may be a great, but temporary decrease. Since the number of educational institutions and the desire for learning and self-betterment are very rapidly increasing, a lasting retrogression in quality and quantity is no longer possible.

The element of abnormality and uncertainty must also be considered in studying the contents of Turkish papers. Since the establishment of the new regime, there has always been some kind of disturbance, such as wars, internal revolts, unsettled political questions, and diplomatic incidents. The papers have had to devote a large part of their space to reporting these extraordinary and disturbing events. Therefore, they do not afford a fair idea, as to what mat-

ters they would give attention and interest to under normal
conditions

There was a period relatively free from disturbing elements, in the time between the Counter-Revolution of April
1909 and the outbreak of the Italian War, (Oct. 1911).
Consequently, this period has been chosen to make a statis-
tical study of the contents of Turkish dailies.

Six papers have been studied, ranging from the governmental *Tanin* to *Sabah* (independent, friendly to government), *Yeni-Gazetta* (independent, friendly to opposition),
Ikdam (moderate opposition), *Alemdar* (opposition), and
Tanzimat (extreme left). The news in about twenty copies
of each has been classified Measurement has also been
made of the amount of space occupied by each class.

The results have been classified in two ways: first into
the paper's own opinion, quoted opinion. entertaining and
instructive feature stories, news, and advertisements; secondly, into various topics according to the nature of the
subjects treated. Both tabulations expressed in relative
figures are given on the following page. These tabulations,
of course, do not show the changes noticeable in the contents of the Turkish papers since the latter part of the year
1911. The changes since that date have included a greater
amount of attention to news from Mohammedan countries,
especially the Turkish provinces in Russia and increased
interest in educational matters Sports, in particular foot-
ball games between Turkish and foreign teams have also
begun to occupy more and more space and attention.

The figures in each of the following tables give the average space devoted to the various classes of printed matter in
about twenty issues of each paper named, expressed as a
percentage of the total space of the twenty copies of each
paper.

TABLE I

General Classes	*Taxin* (Government)	*Alemdar* (Opposition)	*Tanzimat* (Extreme left)	*Ikdam* (Moderate Opposition)	*Yeni-Gazetta* (Independent to Opposition)	*Sabah* (Independent rather Governmental.)
Editorials	6.17%	9.25%	11.20%	6.28%	10.17%	11.74%
Quotations	6 93	8.89	16.72	12.68	6.44	7.17
Special Articles and Fiction	17.92	19.08	14.48	10 85	11.48	12.07
News	45.36	52.72	55.39	43.35	53.46	47.14
Advertisements	23 62	10.06	2.21	26.84	18.45	21.88
	100.00	100.00	100.00	100.00	100.00	100.00

TABLE II

Subject Classes						
World Politics	4.50%	6.49%	15.54%	8.78%	6.25%	5.43%
Turkish external Policy	11.11	8.80	10 15	6.61	9.85	8.90
General internal Policy	4.42	11.28	5.87	11 44	5.52	8 24
Parliament	5.18	4.20	8.09	5.23	4.72	4.40
Party Politics	5.16	11.05	30 47	6.10	1.72	0.58
Internal Unrest	2.37	4 77	4.10	6.46	5.78	4.01
Letters and telegrams from readers on Political Questions	1 84	9.38	5.21	0.56	1.13	0.80
Economics, Industry, Business	2.95	2.85	4.26	3 28	4.26	8.66
Religion	1.04	1.30	0.84	0.49	1.27	0.50
Military	5.40	2.88	2.71	1.15	3.60	1.45
Culture, Science, Education	15.67	10.10	6.16	7.36	14.39	11 95
Court and Society	2.22	1.82	0 28	0.95	3.45	1.23
Criminal and Sensational	2.75	2.96	2.02	3.49	6.36	1.63
Health and Municipality	2.70	3.17	1.56	3 15	4.60	8.55
Various communications from readers	1.26	1.23	0.53	2 48	2.13	2.06
Novel and Fiction	7 81	7.49	....	5 79	6 49	10 59
Governmental Advertisements	8.27	0 95	....	2.33	2.11	3.26
Educational Advertisements	3.38	0.85	0 66	3.09	1 73	3.70
Business Advertisements	11.29	7.69	1.22	21.	14.46	13.31
Personal Advertisements	0.68	0.74	0.33	0.29	0.19	0.74
	100.00	100.00	100.00	100.00	100.00	100.00
Combined length of Columns	750 in.	725 in.	286 in.	760 in.	531 in.	690 in.
Breadth of column	2.65	2.75	2.75	2.57	2.75	2.75

The results of measurements, used according to the formula of solidarity of Professor Giddings, taking all cultural matters (political, economic, educational), political matters, Turkish politics, Turkish internal politics, Turkish party politics as categories, produce the following coefficients of solidarity for the different papers:

	Coefficients of Solidarity	Coefficients of non-Solidarity
1. *Sabah* (independent)	1 31	3 69
2. *Yeni-Gazetta* (independent)	1 38	3.62
3. *Tanin* (governmental)	1.42	3 58
4. *Ikdam* (moderate oppositional) .	1.73	3.27
5. *Alemdar* (oppositional)	2 26	2.74
6. *Tanzimat* (extreme left)	3.17	1.83

The results obtained show that the independent *Sabah* and *Yeni-Gazetta* have no special purpose in view, and are disparate in their contents   The *Ikdam* which inclines to opposition displays a closer firmness of purpose   The *Tanin*, the paper of the majority party, which has to follow a reserved attitude on many questions, does not show quantitively its firmness of purpose.   The proportion suddenly increases with regard to the paper of the opposition party; and a great solidarity and firmness of purpose is seen in the paper of the extreme left.

In spite of their many divergencies in policy and direction, Turkish dailies are alike in their general character and make-up.   They all begin with a signed leading article about two columns long.   Usually, there is a short second article printed in smaller type, on questions of secondary interest.   Then come political news of different kinds, quotations from foreign and provincial papers and letters from correspondents.   The columns preceding the advertisements are occupied by letters from readers, news on cultural matters, on happenings in foreign countries, on new books, and by " short items ", comprising all sorts of police events. Many of these "short items" which are dealt with in three or four lines without any heading, would make very attractive first-page stories for any American paper. The idea of attracting and interesting the reader, at the expense of the professionally accepted standards of dignity would be repulsive to the Turkish journalist.   Not only

crimes and scandals, but also stirring accidents, floods and
fires, do not find access to the first page; in general, not
even to the second page. The " human interest " element
is covered by short stories, special articles and feature
stories translated from foreign papers. Most of the papers
have inaugurated a special feature column, in which events
of actual interest are given humorous and comic treatment
The lower part of the second, sometimes also the third page
is occupied by a novel, or some other kind of serial publication (generally historical essays).

Before the Revolution of 1908, a very limited use was
made of head-lines. Only when an act of the Sultan had to
be given great emphasis was more than one headline used.
There was no type larger than twenty-four point. Wooden
plates had to be engraved for making display on great occasions such as the Sultan's birthday.

' The distaste for more than one headline and the opinion
that more was a vulgar sign of sensationalism continued
for some time after the Revolution But the increase of
competition and expenses, and the succession of important
events, induced the publishers to resort to commercial methods and to disregard old standards in order to interest and
attract the less educated classes of readers For this purpose, larger and larger display types began to be cast.
Since the Balkan War, the use of display types has become
so general that, at times, they are even used to attract attention to editorial articles.

A few years ago such a thing would have been considered,
both by the journalist and the reader, a horrible sacrilege.
Whatever the other parts of the paper might look like the
editorial was expected to be clean, dignified, and free from
every kind of insincerity and sensationalism. It often occurred that the editorial faced a situation squarely and
boldly, while in the news section it was evaded and ignored,

excepting by self-deceiving remarks. The Hellenic agitation among the Ottoman Greeks, for instance, might be
treated by the editorial section in a logical and sincere way,
while, in the news section the information on this matter
was likely to be accompanied by a remark of this sort:
" No word of this can be true, we are convinced of the
loyalty of our Greek fellow-countrymen."

The news editor lacked in many instances the education
which the editorial writer had   Besides he felt obliged to
differ from the attitude of the editorial writer, because most
of the readers had not sufficient understanding for news
published as such. They expected their papers to accompany
all news averse to public feeling with some alleviating comment   The *Yeni-Gazetta* announced repeatedly that it
would give every sort of news in its news section, even if
averse to the policy of the paper and to public feeling,
without any comment, but the experiment did not work and
had to be modified.

Another difficulty the Turkish journalists have, in their
relation with the readers, is in the matter of consistency.
The reader generally expects his favorite paper to be con-
sistent in its views   As a matter of fact consistency is impossible under the pressing and ever-varying stimuli to
which the Turkish journalist is subjected   He cannot take
the view of a cold-blooded on-looker at the situation, when
he sees that so many things dear to him are at stake. Sometimes he has outbursts of pessimism, sometimes he is, on
the contrary, a blind optimist   There are times, when he
makes frank confession regarding the conditions and the
chances of progress of the country; again, he attacks foreign observers bitterly for expressing nearly the same views.
At the bottom of every discussion, he comes invariably to
the question: Can we save ourselves; can we achieve quick
and thorough progress? Some journalists insist upon be-

lieving that a complete and thorough metamorphosis must take place some day, somehow or other; others take a more moderate view.

"I have an unalterable conviction," wrote M. A. Tevfic in the *Tanin*, "that we can be rescued from our inertia and lethargy only by an epoch-making scientific achievement of a Turk. If a Turk makes a great discovery in biology, chemistry, astronomy, or medicine, its stimulating effect on our national pride will be so deep and lasting, that a metamorphosis is likely to take place in our existence. Our intellectual environment will then be changed immediately, and we shall be able to find constructive aspirations in our new generation."

"We ought not to believe in a metamorphosis," answers the *Sabah*. "It is true that we can spare much effort and energy in skipping in many things over different stages of development and adopting at once the final results attained by Western nations. For instance, we can use quinine right away without having to go through the long list of medicines that had previously been used for that purpose. But no kind of metamorphosis can make us understand Nietzsche and Spencer without having a preparatory education."

As these two instances to some extent show, the Turkish journalist inclines to look at things from their most general and fundamental aspect, and from a scientific, at least supposedly scientific, point of view. Although the language of the press has been simplified, in every respect, and the new and practical medium of expression created chiefly by the dailies has swept away the débris of the old and formal phraseology, a new element of complication has been introduced, during the last one or two years by the use of sociological terms even in popular articles. The danger lying in the popular use of such terms is apparent. They serve to cover ignorance and lack of under-

standing, to give authority to misconceived ideas, and to
satisfy the half-educated elements that they have reached
the summit of all learning and scholarship. But, at the
same time, the use made of such terms gives clear evidence
of the general interest taken in social matters and in the
explanation of the social situation. As a result, articles
of a sociological character are taking an increasing space in
reviews and dailies. A large number of sociological works
have been translated from the French, mostly as parts of the
" Free Search " series edited by the publisher of the review
of the same name. There seems to be a large demand for
them, as well as for books written by native authors on
social questions. More than two or three editions of a
sociological work within the space of one or two years is
not a rare event.

Many a reader not only reads passionately what others
say and think, but likes also to see himself in print.
Every day a large number of unsolicited articles pour in at
every newspaper office, dealing with every possible phase
of public interest. There is no pecuniary motive back of
these writings, as Turkish papers never pay for outside contributions, except in cases where contributions are expressly
asked for from well known writers. They are mostly the
work of students, retired officials, militant women, and
reformers of every sort who are sincere in their desire to
advance a new conviction or idea, or of those who simply
wish to see their names in print.

Another class of communication received, expresses the
readers' approval or disapproval of certain opinions of the
paper. A sincere zealous campaign (for instance, in behalf of the peasant class or for non-partisanship in politics)
is sure to bring in a large number of expressions of praise
and sympathy ; poems even, are sent in on such occasions.
On the other hand, a violent and partisan discussion of im-

portant public matters draws critical comments, warnings, and sometimes also anonymous letters of threat.

The press is the first place to appeal to for redress even by those who cannot themselves read. In December, 1910, a group of peasants from a village near Harpout, Asia Minor, came to the office of the *Yeni-Gazetta* to complain that their lands had been taken away by a local boss. The paper immediately opened a campaign against bosses in agricultural communities in general, the one in question in particular. The government made telegraphic inquiries. The accusation was duly denied by the local authorities; still, the peasants came to the newspaper office to give thanks and to say that they felt fully satisfied and redressed because their sufferings and the oppression of the boss had come before the public eye.

Intercourse between readers and papers is not confined to communications, articles, and appeals such as these. Occasionally, inquiries are made among the readers, for instance, as to the best way to celebrate the national holiday, or the ideal persons to govern the country, or the ideal deputy to elect, or the books preferred and read. The *"Tanin"* received in 1910, over two thousand answers to its inquiry as to the best Turkish statesmen from whom to form an ideal cabinet.

Formerly, such inquiries were directed by the editorial department without much thought of business profit. Now, the business department is taking a greater interest in the matter. One of the dailies, (*Tasvir-i-Efkiar*), is distributing prizes with a view to increasing its circulation. This method is resorted to by nearly all of the popular magazines. In fact, the business department is gaining ground at the expense of the editorial department. Not so long ago the editorial staff took great pride in filling the columns with every variety of material which every first-class paper ought to contain according to professional standards, and only the space which happened to be left over was given to advertisements. Now, on the contrary, the editorial staff is becoming obliged to adjust its writing to the amount of advertising matter received, and is coming more and more under the sway of the business manager.

The reason for this change lies, to some extent with the journalists themselves. Owing to the abundance of more remunerative positions in the government service, many of the journalists of ability and prestige have deserted the press since the Revolution. Three have become cabinet ministers, two general governors of provinces, several have obtained positions like general secretaries of provinces. Most of those remaining have given their spare time to parliamentary life, teaching, or magazine writing. Many young men have invaded the field who also have to do some kind of outside work in order to increase their meager salaries. With the exception of the chief and the news editor who receive, on an average, one hundred and fifty dollars and one hundred dollars a month respectively, there are very few men on the staff with a salary of more than fifty dollars. Furthermore, most of the men have very little journalistic spirit, as they begin their careers as translators or re-write men, and not as reporters. No man of any education cares to become a reporter. The reporters who have better developed journalistic instincts than most of the members of the staff, receive as a maximum salary, thirty-five dollars a a month. The average salary is twenty-five dollars a month

Under such conditions, it is no wonder that only a few are able to develop a real attachment to the press and to decide to make journalism their life-work. As a conse-

quence, the professional spirit of the editorial staff and
its prestige and influence with the business department
could not but be declining.

There are, of course, more important reasons than this
for the gaining influence of the business side. They are to
be found in the increasing cost and competition. With
but one exception, all the morning papers are now
stereotyped, and three of them publish pictures. Moreover, no correspondents in the interior are volunteering
their services as they used to do; they expect to be
paid. Competition, as well as patriotic considerations
have induced several papers to keep able traveling correspondents in the interior, in order to report and expose
the existing conditions.[1]

Although the telegraphic agencies are furnishing the
papers with a large amount of foreign news, regular
contributors are maintained in some of the foreign centers for reports, mostly of a cultural character. Competition is further met through special articles, signed by
prominent writers, which are to be paid for and paid for
heavily, as measured by the standards of the Turkish press.

As a result of these expenses and the increasing size,
the papers[2] are sold for less than their cost.[3] Therefore, increasing attention has to be given to advertisements, in order to cover the deficit and secure profit.

[1] The reports sent by Ahmed Sherif, the correspondent of *Tanın*,
exposing mercilessly the deplorable situation in the provinces were published in book form and ran through several editions within two years.
Some of the patriotic readers sent him personal presents, among others,
a gold watch and a fifty dollar bill.

[2] Formerly four pages of the size of the Paris dailies, for the past two
or three years six, sometimes eight, pages of the same size.

[3] The price of the daily is uniformly one cent, or three-quarters of
a cent to the newsboys. Some of the popular weeklies are also sold at
one cent or two   The price of reviews and magazines is from four to
twenty cents.

Among the advertisements, those given by the various state departments have always played an important rôle. The government in power, of course, uses this means to reward support and punish opposition.

Of the papers measured for this thesis and belonging to 1910 and 1911, the organ of the extreme left had no government advertisements at all. The organ of the opposition had only five inches in every number. The independent *Yeni-Gazetta* which was, on certain occasions, strongly oppositional had 12.18 inches, the moderately oppositional *Ikdam* 17.75, the independent *Sabah* 25, and the governmental *Tanin* 62.

Educational advertisements also play a rather important rôle. One or two of eight to twelve advertising columns are occupied by announcements of new books and of different educational institutions. The *École Libre des Sciences Politiques* of Paris and several other French and German schools are accustomed to advertise in the Turkish dailies before the beginning of the school year.

Among the business advertisements, a conspicuous place is taken by those patent medicines which are known to every newspaper reader throughout the world. There are now also native patent medicines which almost go beyond the imported ones in advertising. Department stores, physicians, new Turkish enterprisers and lawyers are also good advertisers. As a result of the agitation made after the revolution the prejudice among Turks against commercial activities has begun to vanish, and to make way for all sorts of business undertakings. Those using their "private initiative" become more and more admired as national heroes. This class of business amateurs often appeals to the national feelings of the readers. One man, a wholesale grocer, has hired permanently the top of the advertising columns of all Turkish dailies to publish each day a short article on the attractions of a business career and " private initiative."[1]

The increasing importance of the advertisements is, of course, bound to end many virtues of the press, which existed during the stage of development, when the satisfaction of the reader and the circulation were the chief concerns of the papers. At that stage, the pressure of the readers' opinions was directly and immediately felt by the paper and a quick adjustment was made necessary.

A few years ago, before the advertiser had become the chief support of the papers, and the political conditions were unsettled, the readers often consciously and formally took advantage of the power of their one cent pieces to punish unpopular or chauvinistic policies of certain papers. The last instance of this sort was in the campaign undertaken by the weekly *Vasifé* (Duty) to have partisan papers boycotted and only independent and moderate dailies read, as long as the former continued their animosity and violence against each other.
"Our cents are a vigorous weapon. Let us save the country from terror by making the right use of them !" was the war-cry used on this occasion.

In the period of violent political agitation, a sudden decline or rise of several thousands was a frequent happening for the papers. The *Tanin*, the *Committee's* organ, for instance, had an average circulation of seven thousand before the Counter-Revolution of 1909. At times, when the *Committee* became very unpopular, it went down as low as four thousand. After the out-

[1] This phrase has been made through repetition, a slogan in the new Turkish era.

break, during which its office was attacked and pillaged, it reached twenty-eight thousand   On account of its using worn out type and a poor quality of paper, it soon dropped to ten thousand.   By enlarging its size, its circulation became fourteen thousand, later eighteen thousand   At the outbreak of the Italian War the circulation was doubled for a few days.   Upon the downfall of the committee government in 1912, the paper immediately lost several thousands of readers

The circulation of the *Ikdam* has also been an exceedingly fluctuating one.   It rose with opportunities to make open opposition, and fell with restrictions made to the liberty of speech.   Its lowest circulation was eight thousand after the troubles of April, 1909.   Fifty thousand copies or more were sold only on special occasions like the outbreak of the Italian War and the publication of an exposé by the late Grand Vezir Kiamil Pasha to justify his attitude during the crisis of December, 1908.   When the *Committee* government fell in 1912, the circulation of the *Ikdam* rose immediately to twenty-six thousand.   This was an increase of thirty per cent.

Since 1912, on account of the wars, the military régime which makes wide deviations from the normal impossible, and the natural elimination of financially weak papers which constituted an element of uncertainty, wide fluctuations have ceased.   Now, all the five morning papers have a circulation close to, or above, fifteen thousand.   As previously mentioned, the amount of circulation gives no indication as to the number of readers, because many of the readers prefer to go to a coffee house, pay one cent (in better located places, two cents) for a cup of coffee or tea, and read all of the dailies and magazines; in addition, they also often borrow the papers of their friends or neighbors.

The extent of coffee-house reading, newspaper bor-
rowing, as well as the individual attitude taken towards
the press were, to some extent, statistically measured
by means of a questionnaire passed around in Constantinople during October, 1913, for the purposes of
this dissertation.   On account of the state of siege permission for this was necessarily obtained from the military authorities.   The questionaires were distributed by
friends of the writer, who, as far as possible obtained
replies from representatives of all classes in the population.   Unfortunately, the group of one hundred and
twenty Turks who filled the questionnaires cannot be
considered fully representative.   Partly because they
feared becoming involved in some kind of trouble, partly
on account of the state of siege, many persons refused
to fill in the questionnaire, although they were expressly
told that they did not have to divulge their identity.

The one hundred and twenty who did answer, with
very few exceptions, took the matter very seriously.
They not only gave long and detailed answers to the
twenty-five points on the questionnaire, but many of
them also ruled the paper carefully and numbered both
the questions and answers   A great number took it as
a good opportunity to give free expression to their
ideas and personality.   Tabulation produces the following results:

Of the one hundred and twenty, one hundred and four
are men and sixteen are women.   The ages differ from
seventeen to sixty, twelve being between seventeen and
nineteen, fifty between twenty and twenty-nine, twenty-
nine between thirty and thirty-nine, fourteen between
forty and forty-nine, and four between fifty and sixty.
Three do not indicate their age.

Forty-three are students or graduates of the law or political science departments of the university, three of them, in addition having studied at the Sorbonne, Paris. The line of study of eight is medicine, of four the military profession, of three theological seminaries, of three commerce (one of them had studied in Vienna), of two agriculture, of two the naval profession. Twenty-two are high school and lyceum graduates, nine grammar school graduates, ten are educated by private tutors, twelve term themselves self-made men. One writes he had almost no education, and one speaks of his education as being "elementary according to the standards of the present century" In addition to Turkish, forty-seven know French, seven French and English, one English, eight French and German, six French and some other native or foreign language, ten some Oriental languages. Forty-one know only Turkish, most of them understanding a little French.

As to their professions, forty-four are state officials, thirteen students, six business men, six teachers, four army officers, four journalists, three lawyers, two theologians, two naval officers, two agriculturalists, two physicians, one an actor, one a mechanic, one a telegrapher, one a politician, one a historian, and one a manufacturer of carving instruments. Ten do not indicate any profession. Some of the sixteen women give their profession as "mothers, the most sacred occupation of all Turkish women," as housewives and as feminists. Three simply answer "they are unfortunately only women," and a seventeen-year-old girl describes herself as an amateur musician.

Forty-six do not belong to any party or society. Twenty-two are strong supporters of the *Committee of Union and Progress*, six are inclined to support the *Committee*, eighteen have their own opinions and ideas, which consist, in the first place, of doing away with party politics. Twelve seem to be in opposition to the present government, six are ready to join a woman's suffrage party as soon as one is inaugurated. Five belong only to non-political societies, one is a socialist, one a pan-islamist, one is a believer in the opinions of the daily *Ikdam*, one in those of the weekly *Ijtihad*, one confesses himself to be a chauvinistic nationalist, although he dislikes the term.

One hundred and thirteen out of one hundred and twenty regularly buy and read newspapers; three buy only when important events take place; three do not buy, but read in coffee houses, one reads only periodicals, and no dailies. Seventy-two regularly read two or more dailies and several periodicals, twenty-five a daily and periodicals eleven only dailies, nine prefer reviews to dailies, three have no regular habit.

Forty-six out of one hundred and twenty go to coffee houses to read papers and also borrow their friends' and neighbors' papers. Thirty-nine exchange their papers with friends who buy other papers, thirty-five read only their own paper.

There are twenty-seven who throw away their papers, or give them to newsboys after reading them. In the average five, in the maximum fifteen or more people, (members of the family, neighbors, friends, relatives in the provinces) take advantage of the papers of the rest.

Seventeen regularly keep, and later have bound, all the papers they buy. Sixty-two conserve papers or extracts from them quite often, but irregularly. Six send them regularly to relatives in the provinces, thirty-five on very rare occasions, or do not conserve papers at all.

In addition, the habit of collecting books is fairly general. For nine it "amounts almost to a craze," for eighteen it is a passion, sixty-eight are interested in collecting books, eighteen have little interest, seven no interest at all.

Forty-three prefer literary works and fiction, thirty-two history, politics and law, twenty-one social sciences, seventeen scientific and professional, and five religious books. One has no choice.

In a month, for papers, periodicals and books, with the exception of school books, four spend less than fifty cents, twelve between fifty cents and one dollar, thirty-three between one dollar and two dollars, thirteen between two dollars and three dollars, four between three dollars and five dollars, and six more than five dollars. Three have no direct expenses, because they go to coffee houses and libraries for reading. Forty-five are not able to make any estimate. An eighteen-year-old student speaks of ninety-five per cent of his pocket money,[1] and two men of six per cent and eleven per cent of their incomes respectively, as used for reading-matter.

Seventeen of those answering fully agree with the views and opinions of their favorite papers. They nearly all state that otherwise they would not read them Thirty-five agree often, thirty-one sometimes, fifteen rarely, six never. For fourteen it is even hateful to think that one might agree with the views expressed in the press. Two do not answer at all.

For fourteen it is a passionate habit to have discussions regarding the views and contents of their papers; thirty-two do it very often, thirty-four sometimes, fifteen rarely, fifteen ordinarily not, ten hate to do it.

[1] This young man is now a student of a high school conducted by French Catholic missionaries. He spends all his money for historical works and intends to become a "religious, learned, zealous and honest Turkish army officer "

The editorial is the part of the paper thirty-four of those questioned read first. Sixty-four begin with the latest news, twelve with fiction and special articles, five with advertisements. Five people do their reading "according to the circumstances."

Forty-two are mostly interested in the political part, thirteen in signed editorials of any kind, twenty-nine in special articles on social problems, ten in matters concerning the progress and welfare of the country, eight in fiction, five in advertisements, two in crimes and sensationalism, one in personal news. Ten have no choice, partly because they cannot find anything of interest in a daily.

Forty-six profit most by the scientific articles on social problems, twenty-one by the editorials, nineteen by news, eleven by business news and advertisements, nine by literary articles and fiction, fourteen have no choice.

The advertisements are read regularly by seventy, sometimes by thirty-seven and very rarely by thirteen.

The new departure of the Turkish press in using numerous and big headlines is welcomed by sixty-one. Nineteen think that the idea is essentially good, but often abused   For thirty it is an unwelcome sign of degeneration and sensationalism. Ten are indifferent to it

The feministic organs published by and for the women have only fourteen warm supporters. Seven think they are not bad. Seven believe in feminism, but find the existing organs too militant. They are, on the contrary, not militant enough for six. Eighteen find them purposeless, fifteen disapprove of them strongly, nine find them dangerous, one of them fearing that "they might make a second Russia out of Turkey". Four think that the place for women is the home. Sixteen have no idea about them and twenty-four have never read them.

Only nineteen out of one hundred and twenty are unconditionally content with the contents of their papers. With exception of nine who do not express any opinion, all the rest think that there are sections in the paper which are needless and should be eliminated. Twenty-eight object to long and tiresome articles, written by incompetent men or translated from foreign papers, which do not reflect any general interest. Nineteen are opposed to polemics, violent attacks on public men, and hot political discussions. Thirteen are opposed to the publication of fiction in serious dailies. Thirteen do not see any need for court, police and personal news. Eleven take exception to advertisements, at least to those of no public benefit. Six think the dailies themselves are superfluous. One is opposed to sporting news, and one is against the use of foreign expressions in the Turkish press

The opinions are more divided regarding the elements which the papers lack. Twenty-eight see the lack in scientific articles and cultural news; seventeen in articles which might serve to enlighten and guide the people; sixteen in business and commercial news; nine in news from distant continents, especially America; six in news from Mohammedan countries; six in articles regarding the rights of women; five in fiction; two in sporting news; one in theatre news, six in general policy and make-up of papers; eight have no special idea, and ten think the Turkish papers are lacking in every essential thing.

The figures given so far cannot fail to indicate how deep an interest the Turkish readers take in their papers, how much they expect from them, and what a single newspaper copy, passed from hand to hand, often read aloud and discussed, in many cases conserved for future reference and reading, is able to achieve.

The present-day achievements of the Turkish press, the increasing specialization in review literature, the attainment of a nearly perfect equilibrium, and of possibilities for constructive work, only after four or five years of contest, struggle and agitation, must be highly surprising to everyone who knows the previous conditions and realizes that there was not even one self-supporting Turkish paper as late as 1860, and that the development of the press between 1876 and 1908 was coercively checked.

For those who take delight in saying that things in Turkey never change, who are only able to see the surface and to think in terms of conventional prejudices, it will not be easy to account for, and to understand, the great and continued changes in Turkey, as indexed and measured in these pages by the development of the press.

In fact there has been taking place in Turkey not too few, but, on the contrary, too many changes. At the beginning of the eighteenth century the old established system was shaken off and began to adjust itself, under various circumstances and auspices, and with varying speed, to new conditions. The price paid was disintegration, territorial loss, arbitrary government, and the appearance of non-social types on both extremes, both among the best, and among the least educated classes.

Now, the imperial burden has been so far lightened, and the destruction of the old order so generally accomplished, that a new era can be ushered in This will be primarily one of capitalistic development, in which surplus will be produced and organized. In the coming era all the disadvantages of an active capitalistic regime will be apparent.   The press in particular will have to forfeit some of its idealism, and some of its virtues.

The advantage to be achieved in return will be stability. And stability is what Turkey needs for obtaining surplus and prestige—two elements which will protect her against foreign invasion and the possibilities of disruption far better than armies and navies be they never so huge.

BIBLIOGRAPHY

The main source of information used in the present study of the Turkish press has been several hundreds of newspaper copies of the period between 1869 and the present day.

When no sources are indicated, many of the statements of a specific character are based upon the general conclusions drawn from these copies, or they are matters of common knowledge to be found in any history of Turkey.

The works used for the different periods are the following·

The Pre-Journalistic Period

Abdurrahman Shereff. *Tarikh-ı-Devlet-i-Osmanié.* 2 vols. Constantinople, 1894 Second ed., 1900.

Catımir, Demetrius. *Histoire de l'Empire Ottoman.* 4 vols. French ed., Parıs, 1743.

Hammer-Purgstall. *Geschichte des osmanischen Reiches.* 4 vols. Sec. ed., Pest, 1834-36.

Jevdett Pasha. *Tarikh-i-Jevdett.* 12 vols. Constantinople, 1855-84.

Loutfi. *Tarıkhi-ı-Loutfi.* Constantinople, 1873-87.

Lybyer, A. H. *The Ottoman Empire in the Time of Suleıman the Magnificent.* Cambridge, 1913.

Mehmed Effendi *Paris Sefartnamessi.* Ebouzzia Edition. Constantinople, 1890.

Moustafa Pasha. *Netayij-ul-vukouhat.* Constantinople, sec. ed, 1911.

Nahıma *Tarikh-ı-Naıma.* Constantinople, 1734. 2 vols, 1863, 6 vols.

Ubıcını, M. A *Letters on Turkey* English ed, London, 1856.

Vassif. *Tarıkh-i-Vassif.* Constantınople, 1805. 2 vols. And Boolak 1827 and 1831.

Zinkeisen. *Geschichte des osmanischen Reiches in Europa.* 7 vols. Hamburg, 1840-63.

The Era of Genesis (1828-1876)

Collas, B. C. *La Turque en 1861.* Paris, 1861.

Dwight, H. D *Turkish Life in War Time.* London, 1881.

Englehardt, E *La Turque et le Tanzimat.* 2 vols. Parıs, 1882.

Gibb. *History of Ottoman Poetry.* 6 vols London, 1900-09

Goodell, Rev William *Forty Years in the Turkish Empire.* New York, 1876.

Horn, P. *Geschichte der turkıshen Moderne.* Leipzig, 1902.

Journal Asıatıque. Paris, July, 1822, Dec, 1827

CPSIA information can be obtained at www.ICGtesting.com
Printed in the USA
LVOW051234230212

270080LV00002B/211/P